Sun Night

E.H. DE LA ESPRIELLA

Printed in the United States of America.

Edited by Samantha Hubbard
Cover, dust cover, book design and collage artwork
by E.H. de la Espriella
Published by Enrique de la Espriella
Photography by Sonia Ortiz and James Peshek

2023 Re-release.

ISBN: 979-8-9868692-5-4 Hardback
ISBN: 979-8-9868692-4-7 Paperback

Learn more at SunNightBook.com.

To my brother, Luchi.

The Clouds Above

When I was a child, I saw clouds in the bedroom ceiling. I saw them. I did. I shared that bedroom with my brother, but he never saw the clouds. I don't know why he didn't, and I didn't question it because there were bigger questions about life that needed to be answered first. Questions about what it means to live and what it means to die. What it means to love another human being and what it means to see them leave. In this room with clouds above, we shared our ideas, thoughts, stories, feelings, suffering, and happiness. In this room, we supported each other when we felt lonely and helpless.

The clouds were spinning, swirling with no sign of stopping. Gray, foamy, puffy; the clouds moved in a vortex and didn't travel anywhere else. From corner to corner, and from one end to the other of the ceiling, the smoky clouds moved violently, appearing like an approaching storm. From time to time there were sparks and flashes of light filling the swirls. The clouds churned in the ceiling of the bedroom that Sebastian shared with his brother Santiago.

Sebastian, who was in bed with his covers pulled up to his neck, moved his right arm from under the sheets and shielded his eyes from the menacing billows above him. Suddenly, very small dots of different colors began to emerge from the bedroom ceiling. Slowly, the vicious foam of clouds began to disappear as if by magic. Night had come and all went quiet in the room. Sebastian's eyes felt heavier. He moved his arm back under the sheets and fell completely asleep.

Morning came and light began to fill the room where Sebastian and Santiago slept. It was a simple apartment room with large sliding closet doors and two single beds separated by a wood night table painted white. Sunlight began to fill the room and color appeared on the closet doors where Mickey, Minnie, Donald, and Goofy characters had been painted by their mother in a weekend project months before. The beds, the sheets, the covers, and the pillows were all the same for each brother; simple half inch stripes of white and yellow.

More of the room became visible by the light and small matching desks emerged against the wall near the door to the hallway, opposite the closet doors. The wall, ceiling, and doors were all white; bone white, as their mother called it. The only decorations on the walls, aside from the characters on the closet doors, were above the night table; two pictures depicting clowns with big sad eyes looking out toward the windows. There was also a clown lamp on the night table, and a square clock with glow-in-the-dark numbers. Under the night table, in the cabinet below, were storybooks, with the front one titled *The Water Babies*.

The door of their room opened at 6:20, like it did every school day morning. A woman in her mid-thirties entered the room. She was their mother, and her name was Michelle. She was beautiful, tall, and slim, with brown hair and eyes, and silky white skin. She was ready for work in a brown dress, a color very popular in the seventies. She told the boys to open their little eyes and to wake up to get ready for school. She was pleasant and loving to her kids. Michelle stopped by each of their beds. First by Santiago's bed, the one closest to the door. Sebastian, the older and always the most somber and responsible of the two, got up first and ran to the bathroom in his pajamas. Michelle started to fix Sebastian's bed while trying to get Santiago to rise from his sleep.

Sebastian, still sleepy, relieved himself and then took a look at his reflection in the mirror above the sink while brushing his teeth. An 11-year old boy looked back at him, alone and without any idea what the future held for him. Within the year, his life was going to change completely. Sebastian was pale with dark hair and big brown eyes that appeared almost black. He hoped he would one day grow into his teeth, as they appeared almost too big for his head. Sebastian was the introvert; very shy, sensitive, and quiet, preferring to be neither seen nor heard. Sebastian was scared of everything; the whole world around him; and a total contrast to his brother Santiago who was loud, outgoing, and friendly to even the strangest of strangers.

Santiago was full of life; always running, jumping, and meddling in others' business. Sebastian was two years older than Santiago, and recognized the responsibility of being an older brother. He always took the role of teacher, which happened to be their mother's profession. Santiago was shorter with dirty blonde hair and green eyes that changed color depending on his mood or how strongly the sun was shining that day.

Sebastian and Santiago came from a middle-class family where both parents worked. Their father Esteban, a hospital laundry manager, was a heavier man always perspiring from the constant Panamanian heat and humidity. Stockier in shape, he was much taller than his wife, and even though he was also white, his skin tone was darker than hers. With an army haircut and strong Italian features, Esteban could have been mistaken for European in those days.

Like a recorded message, the trip to school was the same every day; Michelle packed her two kids into the back of her 1974 bright yellow Volkswagen Beetle, picked up a neighborhood kid who was much older than her own children and that went to the same school. This gave Michelle an additional means of income. She drove through the streets to get to the school where she taught English as a second language.

Once at the school, she would park the VW in the same parking spot reserved for teachers. The neighbor girl who always sat in the front seat would get out first, then Michelle, and finally the boys, who would emerge from the back seat. Santiago jumped on his mother and gave her a big kiss while pulling her down to his height. Sebastian followed his brother. Everyone said goodbye to each other and were all on the way to their individual classrooms.

Then, as the day fast-forwarded, everything repeated in reverse. Everyone reconvened in the same spot, jumped into the Volkswagen and returned home.

After dinner that evening, the kids did their homework on the dining room table while their father tried to fix the light switch in the kitchen. He was sweating as usual, only wearing an undershirt and the only black slacks he appeared to own. The children could hear the click of the light switch repeatedly but nothing changed. There were still no lights. Their dad hovered over the light switch as if trying to decipher a hieroglyph, and wondered what was so unusual that the switch wouldn't work properly.

"A transformer." Screamed Michelle. "Could it be that a transformer burned?"

Esteban hadn't even thought of it, and looked at her with a smirk. He disappeared to the back room behind the kitchen where the fuse box was located. They heard some rattling noises, and a minute later he reappeared with his hands grabbing the kitchen towel and wiping the sweat off his neck and face. He flipped the switch once more and the kitchen light turned on. He was elated for someone that seldom showed much emotion.

That night, they sat in front of the television set on the dark blue rug in front of their parents' bed, watching *The Topo Gigio Show*. Sebastian gazed at the mouse on the screen while trying to figure out how he could move so lifelike. Both watched while trying not to blink, in order to avoid missing a moment of it. The show ended as it always did, where Topo Gigio was ready for bed. And as he always did at the end of every show, he yawned dramatically and said "to the bed, to the bed." in a race to see if he or the presenter would say it first. Then he proceeded, "I said it first, I said it first," singing in an adorable innocent manner. Sebastian and Santiago, with big smiles on their faces, recited the words at the same time with Topo Gigio. Both boys, who were lying on the floor on their stomachs, got up and stretched mimicking the movements Gigio acted out on the screen. They continued to watch for the presenter to say good night to Gigio and the program ended. Their father wished them a good night as the children reluctantly shuffled to their bedroom.

At eight o'clock, Sebastian and Santiago were in their beds, already in their pajamas. It was Thursday night, one more day of school before the weekend. The night was warm and humid, but that was normal in Panama City. The oscillating fan was already working hard on the middle speed setting. Michelle checked on them minutes later, before turning the light out in their bedroom.

"Have a good night my sweets and dream with angels." She told them, as she always did.

Santiago seemed chatty that evening, telling Sebastian about his schoolmate Roger that got into trouble in school earlier that day.

"Can you believe Roger cursed in Spanish class today? Mrs. Sanchez was furious. And he didn't show any remorse; he was just staring at her with a smile as if it was the funniest thing in the world. He couldn't even hold back the thrill of doing something so funny."

Santiago actually felt bad for Mrs. Sanchez because she had recently divorced and didn't smile much after that. Not like he knew what the word divorce meant, but he was sure it wasn't a good thing. Santiago and Sebastian didn't ask for details because they really didn't want to know the horrible truth of it all. All they knew was that it was something bad; something people didn't talk about around the children, based on the expressions, shifts in conversation, and rolling of eyes from their parents every time the subject would come up.

Sebastian laughed as Santiago blurted out the four-letter word mimicking how Roger would have sounded when he said it in class. Sebastian then changed the subject and told Santiago about his day and how physical education class was tedious because he disliked sports and was obligated to play soccer with the other kids in order to get a passing grade. Once the boys were on the soccer field, they had to play until they made their physical education uniforms dirty. Sebastian would always pick to play goal defense so that he didn't have to run around and get tired like the other kids did. When the ball would come in his direction, he would fall on the dry reddish-brown earth and roll around until his green shorts faded to the same color of the dirt.

By this time, Santiago was half way between here and there and wasn't responding much to Sebastian's story. All you could hear in the room was Sebastian talking quietly in Santiago's direction on the bed next to him.

After a while, Sebastian turned his head and looked up into the ceiling of their room. The clouds were swirling around up in the ceiling again. They were grayish blue this time, and grayish purple in some places. Dots of different colors appeared on the ceiling and suddenly disappeared. Sebastian rubbed his eyes with his fingers and wondered if Santiago could also see them. He also wondered why they only came out during the night. This phenomenon was there, it was vivid and alive. The boy closed his eyes and continued to see disappearing dots inside of his eyelids. He opened them again to see what else would show on the ceiling of his room.

A car with loud music drove by the building, loud enough to be heard on their third-floor apartment room. The music playing was a loud boom sound, maybe a Donna Summer tune with very low bass, hard to define from the distance. The lights from the passing car reflected, duplicated, and multiplied into the room bringing some of the light that was now a field of colorful rainbow effects casting on to the ceiling. The clouds were still there, circling in a never-ending maelstrom. Sebastian then heard Santiago turn in his bed to look away; perhaps the music and the lights coming into the room bothered him. Sebastian covered himself tightly to keep himself protected from anything coming down from the ceiling that may want to grab him or do harm because in the end, he still didn't fully trust it. He knew that Santiago was safe when he was asleep, so he didn't worry about him being in danger.

"Santiago, I need to go pee." Sebastian called to his brother without a response. Santiago was deeply asleep. Sebastian called on his brother once more, this time loudly.

"Santiago, wake up, I really need to go pee!" He glanced at the time on their bedside table. It was 2:15 in the morning. Santiago moved in his bed, bothered by his brother's roaring call. Sebastian got up slowly, making sure to stay covered under his bed sheet, and extended his right arm over to Santiago's bed to push him and wake him up.

"Santiago, I need to go pee. Come with me." Sebastian asked desperately. His brother finally opened his eyes and asked his older brother what he wanted.

"You need to go on your own. There is nothing in the hallway." Responded Santiago to his frightened brother who did this almost every night. The hallway looked darker than night itself but he could still see glimpses of the door changing shape from his point of view. He looked without blinking as if expecting a freak image to appear from the door. He could see a soft light glow around the door playing games with Sebastian's eyes and made him see the door change from a rectangle to a square and then to a circle and slowly it started to take the shape of a face. Sebastian was so completely intimidated by what his eyes were showing him that he even started to hear noises that weren't there.

Santiago rose up from his bed, eyes closed, and extended his hands to pull his brother off his bed. All the while, the door to the hallway was transforming in front of Sebastian's eyes. Santiago grabbed his brother's hand and pulled him out of his bed. They walked slowly and carefully, Sebastian following behind his brother toward the door that had now returned to its original shape. Santiago opened it and both walked through to the bathroom, which was only a couple of steps away from their bedroom door. Sebastian looked around for anything odd, but everything seemed to be normal as it usually was. They got to the bathroom and Sebastian ran toward the toilet and relieved himself while Santiago stood outside, eyes closed, facing the living room. They both heard a distant noise. Santiago opened his eyes but didn't notice anything, then called for his brother.

"Aren't you done yet?"

Sebastian answered by flushing the toilet and running back outside. He held Santiago's hand as they walked back to their bedroom, Sebastian entering their bedroom first, leaving Santiago behind to close the door. He then separated from his brother and jumped from Santiago's bed to his own. The bedroom door was only partially closed so Sebastian asked his brother to push the door closed shut, otherwise Sebastian could not imagine leaving the door open for even one minute the rest of the night. Both in their beds, Sebastian covered himself to his nose, while

Santiago hardly covered at all, both falling asleep.

It was Friday morning, at last. The sun was shining brightly. Fridays were culture and arts days at the boys' school. While Sebastian looked forward to the day because of the opportunity to use his artistic skills, Santiago thought doing art was a waste of time. It was not that he didn't like art or culture; he just didn't find it as appealing and exhilarating as his older brother did. If Santiago was given an option, he would choose sports every time.

In the last class of the day, Sebastian had to create something made out of magazine clippings, an introduction to collage. They had been studying the planets in science class and in this particular week they discovered the power of the sun. This inspired Sebastian to cut out sections from an old magazine with bright colors and glue them to a piece of 8 by 10 poster board. He pasted different colors, from lightest to darkest, in a repetitive pattern that expressed the shooting of light from the center outward to the edges of the surface. It was something that reminded him of the flashes of light he had seen in the ceiling of his room. For an eleven-year-old child, the work was quite mature and his teacher could tell there was something special about it. The kids had one hour to put together their work, and he was one of the last ones to finish due to the amount of work involved. Sebastian felt satisfied of what he had accomplished that day.

At home that evening, Michelle and the kids had sandwiches for dinner with small salads as they usually did on Friday nights.

Esteban was never around on Fridays. Or Wednesdays. Or Saturdays. In the last few years, their dad went out after work to drink with his friends. The kids felt a certain uncomfortable environment every night of these drinking outings. They really didn't understand what was going on, but knew something wasn't right.

Michelle seemed distant and concerned about something that evening, but the conversation at the table helped to distract her with thoughts of other things. Sebastian and Santiago always discussed the day's events at the dinner table, and if they didn't bring it up, their mother usually did. This day wasn't any different, other than the kids could feel the consternation in their mother's mind. Santiago reached out to get the salt for his salad and spilled the orange drink from his cup all over the table. The loud bang of the plastic cup pounding on the wood tabletop shook his brother and mother.

"Not again Santiago, you have to be more careful." Yelled out Michelle as she quickly ran to the kitchen to fetch a cleaning cloth to help absorb the spill. By the time she got back to the dining room, the kids had taken ten paper napkins and scattered them all over the table to soak up the spilled soda. The napkins were drenched, and as Michelle pulled them inward to the center of the table to avoid the liquid spill onto the floor, she loudly said, "San, San, San, what are we going to do with you? You have hands made out of cloth or something!"

Sebastian smirked while looking at his brother, then took a bite off of his almost gone salad. By the time Michelle was back from washing off the kitchen towel, the kids were chatting about the school project Sebastian had worked on earlier that day. He told his mother and sibling about the collage he had to create and that he didn't know what that was until the teacher shared some examples. Michelle then asked Sebastian to tell them all about it. He explained that he not only enjoyed it but he also found the subject of science to be quite fascinating, and this helped him explain easily all the things he had learned about the sun. Santiago asked Sebastian to tell him more about the sun. Sebastian continued with a smile and responded, "The sun is millions of miles away and it is a star like all the other stars we see in the night." He went on and on for two or three minutes, while his brother finished chewing on his salad.

By now, Michelle had refilled Santiago's glass with orange soda and asked Sebastian to show them the brilliant artwork he had created.

He ran to his bedroom and pulled the collage carefully out of his school bag. He noticed that a corner had been dinged, and straightened it back, trying to flatten it to its original place. He walked back, complaining to his mom that the corner had been damaged when he was taking it out, but she told him not to worry about it. Sebastian was quite happy with what he had done and thought he should have just been a little bit more careful. He pulled up the artwork on the table, making sure that the top was already dry to avoid damaging it. He placed the sheet with sun rays emanating from the center facing his mother and brother, while studying the expression on their faces.

Michelle took the collage and let out a delighted shout of enjoyment. "This is so pretty, Seb! What did the teacher say when she saw it?"

He replied that everyone liked it. Santiago enthusiastically told his brother what a great job he did. Sebastian ran back to their bedroom to hang the artwork on the wall above his bed.

That evening, they all settled in to their routines. The kids did their homework so that they could enjoy their weekend without having to think of school. Having Michelle as a teacher taught the boys good behavior, discipline, and responsibility. Sebastian had to do more homework about the sun, which involved writing a short essay on solar effects on earth. Once he was finished, the kids watched television and by 8:30 they were yawning and feeling sleepy. It was already 30 minutes past their bedtime anyway, but because it was Friday, Michelle allowed them a little more time to be with her.

At times, she seemed withdrawn and her children had been noticing this behavior in her for some time, and thought that maybe she was worried about them or their father. Their dad was always working or going out, not very present in their lives, and perhaps she stressed over that. They could only assume this, as they didn't understand the complexities of adult relationships and marriage; only the bits and pieces they heard from their school friends.

Where Does the Sun Go at Night?

When my brother and I were young, we fantasized about whatever we could think of when the lights went out in our bedroom at night. We talked about dreams, our realities and how we were going to change the world when we grew up.

The night was tranquil and quiet; there were no loud cars running through the street, which was unusual for a Friday night. It was cloudy with a chance of rain that evening, perhaps it was the reason for the quietness in the air. Distant lightning could be seen, accompanied by a light humid breeze. Sebastian and Santiago changed into their pajamas and jumped in their respective beds, but not before Sebastian took a minute to admire the collage above his bed. It brought a breath of fresh air into the stark white wall, but clashed harshly with the cartoon characters painted on the closet doors. Sebastian got into bed first, followed by his brother. Michelle turned the light out in the bedroom after giving each a kiss on their cheeks. She was unusually quiet. The door closed behind her and the room went dark.

In unison, both Sebastian and Santiago turned to face each other, and with wide eyes began to chat again as they always did. Sebastian talked to Santiago about the essay he had to write, and that he didn't know how everything could work so well together on earth and the planets. There was obviously scientific knowledge beyond their comprehension, but it left them both enamored with the idea that there was more to life than what they knew, and they were both excited to open their minds to learn more about the mysteries of the universe.

A couple of minutes went by when there was complete silence; perhaps they had both fallen asleep. Sebastian had his eyes closed as if he were completely checked out. Then Santiago blurted out softly as if not to disturb his brother. "Where does the sun go at night?"

After a moment of deep thinking, Sebastian answered, "What do you mean? Where does the sun go? The sun is always there!"

"No, when the sun goes down at the end of the day, where does it go?" Santiago quickly responded.

Sebastian smiled, even chuckled a little. "The sun goes over to the other side of the earth," said Sebastian.

His brother replied, "But where?"

Remembering the decorative Asian vases that their parents had displayed around the house, Sebastian said, "The sun pops up on the other side of earth in China."

"I don't understand how it can go all the way over there." Santiago inquired.

"Well, Santiago, once the sun pops out from our side, it just pops in on the other side." Santiago could picture the Chinese horizon with silhouettes of pine trees and the sharp vertical architecture with curved roofs illustrated on the Chinese vases, the sun peeking out just a bit, then popping up into the sky as if a large hand had pushed it there. The force of the movement of the giant ball of fire caused the clouds around it to move up and away from it, some dissipating from the impact altogether.

Then he continued to listen to his brother telling him what happened when the sun went to the other side.

"The sun shoots light rays on rice fields where men and women with pointy round straw hats work on the land. Then it moves the rays to the tall pointy mountains with an incredible range of color, from grayish blue and rising to a lighter almost pinkish color at the peaks. The sky is equally alive, but with a contrasting range of coloration beginning with a very light green near the surface of the earth and moves upward to a lighter powder blue." Santiago could even feel the texture of the man-made paper in his mind.

"The clouds complemented the color of the sky." But these clouds were different than the clouds menacing in the approaching storm of that evening. The cloud shapes were unusual and, he recalled, very similar to the ones in the vase behind the sofa on the display table. Sebastian told him that a large hand came into the center of each individual cloud and with the index finger started to swirl the cloud in a circular fashion, creating whirlpools in the sky all over the Asian territories that lay in the path of the sun.

Sebastian then began to tell him about the Chinese boys and their father. "They are playing on the top of one of the mountain peaks close to the sky. It is a beautiful clear day, with a cool breeze that seems to pick the kids up in the air, moving them in harmony side by side with their matching gold and red attire. The boys are running around a green uneven field on top of a hill, while their dad pulls two red kites with long tails out of his travel bag. The kites are made out of light thin paper and balsa wood sticks, hand-made by him to give to his kids as a gift for earning good grades in school." Sebastian told Santiago that once they saw the kites, the children started to jump up as if they could fly.

"They jumped like cartoon characters, bouncing slowly as if the air was thicker and made them fall slower than normal, so high above the clouds. The children were young, younger than us, and they had not yet learned how to fly kites, but they had seen other kids fly them in the past, at the town's yearly kite competition show."

Santiago could imagine the brothers listening to their dad explain how to pull the kites up in the air, as he tried to demonstrate for them.

"He rolled a little bit of the cord attached to the kite

and loosened some of the line, which allowed the first kite to hang slightly off his hands. He then tried to feel the air moving around him, to get the direction of the wind, and pulled the kite as he walked hurriedly away from the kids. Nothing happened. The man tried two more times with the same kite, repeating the same motions, but the breeze kept pulling against him. The father began to perspire. The anger and disappointment showed on his face, and he looked down ashamed that he was unable to complete such an easy task. He had done this so many times before when he was a young boy himself, but perhaps because of his age and weight he was unable to in front of his children. As he looked over at his kids, he held back his feelings of shame for disappointing them. He tried once more, now with the other kite. With one last glimpse of hopeful anticipation, he was knocked off by a stone in the path of his left foot and fell forward to the ground. The kite he had been pulling started to take off quietly in the air as if the fall accelerated its departure. It started to move up and up toward the sky bouncing from the left to the right in a slow, wavy motion. The sun was in the way and all the father could see was the silhouette of the kite as it swayed back and forth in the sun's path. It began to head toward the ground with increasing speed, the tail ceremoniously following the body of the kite, closing the distance toward the father until, with considerable speed, it came down and broke into three pieces on top of him. The father closed his eyes and raised his left hand, which had been holding the knee he banged in the fall, to protect himself from the falling kite. As all of this was happening, the kids were running behind their dad, hoping and yearning for the kite's successful launch, suddenly stopping in their tracks in complete shock. The kids looked at each with their mouths open in astonishment. The older boy grabbed his brother's hand and ran toward their dad to check to see if he was alright. As they approached him, they could tell that he was visibly hurt and upset. The children asked their dad if he was injured, but he didn't answer back. Slowly he got up and with his wounded leg he kicked the broken paper kite, breaking it into even more parts. He was disappointed and upset, and walked quickly, as fast as he could with his damaged leg, back to put the destroyed kite and the other items back into the bag. The father then packed all the loose items and some uneaten plums he had brought on the kite journey. Once all the items were packed away, the father announced to his boys that they were returning home, but he never looked at them as he told them this. The children bowed their heads out of respect, while sorrow reflected on their faces. And down the tall mountain they went, in parts almost vertically, through naturally chiseled ladders in the hard rock. The sun withdrew from the sky behind the upright range, and the father, children, and the scene went completely obscure. Then the sun moved slowly ahead toward the ocean and with a swirling motion lowered in the sky. The clouds moved just as gradually away from the sun. The water of the sea pushed away from the pressure of the sun descending into the large expanse of ocean as if it didn't want to feel the burn. Then, the orange swirls that surrounded the perfectly round yellowish-white shape that forms the light that gives us life, pushed in firmly as if its existence depended on it. The sun ultimately made contact with the water and it boiled and evaporated from the extreme heat. The sun suddenly popped into the water the same way it popped back into China earlier that day."

"You're funny, Sebastian." Said Santiago to his brother while laughing quietly. "That could never happen, really!"

To which Sebastian responded, "You never know!"

The brothers talked for a little while longer. The rain had moved into the city now. Santiago covered himself with the thin covers as if it was freezing cold outside. Sebastian, already covered, turned to face the ceiling of their bedroom. Both heard a noise coming from the hallway outside their door, and both closed their eyes. The door of their room opened slowly as Michelle walked in, already in her nightgown. She didn't say a word, expecting that her children were asleep. She closed the windows so that rain wouldn't come in the room. In the same expeditious manner, she disappeared behind the door. Both Sebastian and Santiago continued to keep their eyes closed until she left walked out.

After a couple of minutes and once they were assured that all movement outside the hallway had abated, Sebastian continued, "Santiago, do you ever see clouds in the ceiling?" But he didn't get a response.

"Santiago!" He quietly called again, but no answer. He deduced that his brother was fast asleep or faking it, which he sometimes did when his mom would walk in the room. Sebastian pulled himself up on his bed and looked over at his brother, but Santiago was now turned toward the door away from him and was completely still. Sebastian relaxed back in his bed, and pulled his covers a little bit higher covering himself over his nose, so that only his eyes were exposed. He closed his eyes and sighed, ready to fall asleep. But he couldn't help opening his eyes again and checking out what the ceiling had in store for him this time. The clouds were there as they always were, circulating as usual. The central vortex showed remnants of a light source. It was slowly being swallowed into the center and into the deepest regions of the ceiling. After the light disappeared, the clouds turned darker and more ominous. They slowly dissipated as if a ghostly black hole were sucking up all life. Sebastian closed his eyes and went to sleep.

BANG! THUD! CRASH! At 1:30 in the morning, the children were awakened by unexpected loud noises coming from outside of their bedroom. Sebastian opened his eyes wide and scared, ready to scream, while Santiago just looked over at his brother, wondering what was going on. They heard people screaming.

"Why are you just getting home now?" Asked the female voice. Something else slammed onto a wall and made a shattering sound.

"Shut up!" Screamed the male voice. The boys stayed in their beds, just looking at the door to the hallway, expecting that it would open at any minute. Santiago waited to hear more of his parents' voices and suddenly got out of bed and ran to the door to turn the lock so that their parents couldn't come in the room. They continued to hear their parents shout at each other for some time. Michelle was furious with her husband.

"I was at the bar all this time." He yelled in defense.

"I called the bar and all I could hear was loud music playing and they said you were not there! Where were you?" Shrieked Michelle as loud as she possibly could.

"I was there!" It was his only response. Then he said, "Shut up and go to sleep. All you do is complain about what I am doing."

"I can't go to sleep now, until you tell me where you have been." She replied defiantly.

Bang! Something else dropped on the floor, perhaps not intentionally this time, and everything went quiet. The boys were still sitting in their respective beds and looking at each other imagining the scene outside their door. Their parents' bedroom door slammed, and a terrified Santiago jumped from his bed into Sebastian's. Then the kids heard what they thought was the front door of the apartment open and slam shut. After a few minutes, they heard the faint sounds of sobbing. The kids were so scared now, and took comfort in holding each other, their arms wrapped around one another in love and fear.

"Santiago, you didn't get to hear what happened to the sun when it got back to our side."

Santiago was not even paying attention to his brother,

still concerned for what had just happened.

"What?" Asked Santiago.

Sebastian spoke quietly so that their mother wouldn't hear them. "I was telling you about the sun, remember? Well, the sun was just starting to push into the ocean water and remember some of it was burning off."

Santiago responded, "Yes, but I don't remember what happened after that."

Sebastian continued, "Well, that is because the sun had taken you into its spell. The sun was using his rays to hypnotize you in the same way it had the kids on the top of that mountain."

Santiago wiped a tear off his cheek and proceeded to ask his brother in a small quiet voice, "So where did the sun go after that?"

Sebastian recalled the type of food he liked most and responded, "It went to Italy." Remembering their great grandmother's home town in Italy he continued.

"There, the sun was furiously warming the people at this little town called Castrovillari. The rolling mountains in that region were very green and the people of the town were all very happy to welcome the sun every morning, but especially that morning."

Santiago's mind imagined how the sun touched the

skin of the Italians in that little town.

"The townspeople were dressed in clothes that looked like those people in the renaissance art book our parents have on top of the coffee table. Remember the light red dresses lined in gold the women wore? The women and girls had equally golden curls, and the men and boys wore green shorts and white shirts, like our school uniforms. And they seemed to be celebrating and dancing in the center of town. It happened to be olive picking season and all the families of town geared up for the festival of lights they celebrated every year before they picked the first olives off the trees. The sun was dancing with them as well. It moved in a circular shape creating a ring of fire that could be seen all over town. Even the birds flying seemed to dance along an almost musical sound wave that was carried by the breeze all around them. Suddenly everyone, all at once, lifted white square handkerchiefs in the air and moved them in a circular fashion above their heads, all in harmony to the music playing in the background. It made even the olive trees seem as if they were moving to the same tune with the people around them. The earth trembled from the pressure of all the townspeople walking toward the olive groves. Then after all this delight, the sun moved behind a layer of clouds which broke off the fire ring into several parts. The people below quieted down. They slowed down their movements and lowered themselves close to the ground where they grabbed their empty olive baskets, and in the same way they had danced moments earlier, they rose up and began to work in unison. The handmade straw containers they all held had intricate designs of the region. The villagers passed them to the other men and women that stood in a line down the hill to the olive fields. With gloves protecting their hands, the men raised wooden ladders and stepped up toward the sky and into the trees where they shook the branches to detach the black, oval, crisp fruit. They passed bunches of olives to the children below them. And they smiled and ran from one side of the olive tree farm to the other in a repeating pattern, like a marching band stepping in sync. A couple in love teased each other as they tossed olives at one another. All the seniors of the town sitting up on top of the hill could see swirls created by flying olive bunches that traveled from one side to the other of each tree creating bewitching curvilinear patterns in the air above. The action was almost spiritual like the peppery flavor of the first squeeze of the olive harvest."

Santiago exclaimed while yawning, "What happened next, Seb?"

"Shh!" Replied Sebastian to avoid their mom hearing

them chat in their bedroom.

"After a whole day of work, the families returned to the center of town to bring in all the fruit they had acquired. By now, the sun had released itself from the circular dance above the town and had started its journey from Italy into France and Spain. The Castrovillarians lit torches and placed them on white marble column posts around the mountain of olives that mimicked the mountains surrounding the town."

Sebastian waited a moment and looked down at his brother who was now next to him lying down in the bed with his eyes closed.

"Santiago?" Called Sebastian to his brother. He was met with silence. Sebastian got up quietly and moved over to his brother's bed. He got in the bed and covered himself, exhausted from the screaming and tension of that night. Tears started to roll down his cheeks as he turned to see his little brother in his bed. And his body began to shake from the cold of night, the dark of the space, the unjustified aggression in their home, and the feeling that he was completely helpless. He took one more glance at the time; it was now 3:34 am and he closed his eyes.

Both brothers woke up around 8:30 and looked around,

baffled as to why they were sleeping in the wrong beds, and quickly reminding themselves of what had transpired earlier that morning. Sebastian unlocked the door and walked carefully out into the hallway to find that nothing seemed out of place. The bathroom door was closed and sounds were coming from the other side. He knocked on the door and asked to use the bathroom. He heard the sound of his mother's voice behind the door cheerfully responding, "Yes, honey, I'll be right out."

Sebastian returned to his bedroom and sat on Santiago's bed looking out into the hallway, patiently waiting for the door of the bathroom to open. Santiago just stared up at the ceiling with a blank expression as he was just starting to awake from his restless sleep. Once the door of the bathroom opened, Michelle appeared in the hallway dressed up in her favorite red polka dot one-piece dress but without any shoes. With a towel in one of her hands, she looked into her kids' room and softly asked them if they slept alright. The boys could tell she felt guilty about the early morning yelling and door slamming commotion. She appeared a bit fatigued as if she had not slept all night, and perhaps she never did, but she walked in and gave them each a big hug in an attempt to protect their tender hearts and comfort her guilt. Sebastian ran to the bathroom, overjoyed that his mother was acting normal, while Santiago and his mom stayed in the room chatting.

There was something different about this Saturday morning; their dad was nowhere around. After the usual morning grooming and bedroom organizing, Michelle prepared breakfast for the kids but all throughout that time, Michelle looked pensive and extraordinarily quiet. Once the scrambled eggs, bacon, and tortillas were plated, she called the kids into the dining room and sat them down in their usual spots. Conversation was light this morning. The kids wanted to avoid the subject about the previous night. Halfway through the meal, the master bedroom door opened and their dad emerged from the cold dark room. Santiago even felt the cool breeze coming into the dining room from his parents' air-conditioned bedroom. No one said a word. Esteban walked quietly into the kitchen as if no one were in the house. As his figure disappeared through the door to the kitchen, both Sebastian and Santiago deliberately looked over at their mom in unison to inspect the reaction on her face, but soon enough their dad walked backwards into the room after registering that his family was sitting together having breakfast. Their dad looking only at his kids, wished them a good morning, and gave them a brief but awkward smile. His face looked tired, with deep bags under his eyes and red blotchy veins, as if he had survived a terrible accident. He was wearing a faded white T-shirt and his favorite house shorts. He then disappeared into the kitchen again. Michelle smiled civilly at her kids and finished up her last bite of tortilla. In a swift and graceful movement, she stood up and took her plate, fork, and knife into her hands and walked into the kitchen. The children continued to eat their food, but very quietly this time, trying to hear what was happening on the other side of the wall. The parents chatted quietly as if telling a secret to one another, then a moment of stillness was followed by the surprising appearance of Santiago into the kitchen, holding his dirty plate and silverware. He stopped in front of his parents holding his plate up high and looked up with the same eyes as those in the clown pictures in his bedroom wall. Michelle grabbed the plate and other items from his hands and thanked him.

Santiago looked at his dad and asked him, "How are you doing, dad?"

His dad replied with a smile, "Okay, son." Santiago turned around and ran out of the kitchen.

Later that afternoon, their father arrived home after being out most of the day. The kids never found out where he'd been. He continued to act detached from his family.

Both Sebastian and Santiago had been watching a TV program they were very fond of on Saturdays, and which was just ending, when their father walked in the room. He changed into his house clothes and went into the kitchen to get a rum and coke. It appeared to the children that their parents had made up because they were talking once again. After dinner, Michelle asked the kids to be on their best behavior because they would be entertaining some friends that evening.

That night in bed, they could hear their parents' spirited voices chatting with their friends. There was laughter and the noise of glasses striking the surface of the glass coffee table in the living room. Sebastian wasn't as talkative that evening so Santiago asked him what was the matter.

Sebastian responded, "Today was weird."

Santiago agreed. His brother continued, "I wish dad wouldn't drink. He turns weird when he does, and I don't like it when he does. I get scared."

Santiago responded, "I know, I get scared too. But don't worry, Seb."

Sebastian sighed and stayed quiet for a while. They continued to hear the sounds of their parents and friends chatting in the distance. They could only distinguish a few familiar words here and there.

After a while, Santiago asked Sebastian about the sun and where it had gone that night. Sebastian may have not been paying attention because he asked his brother to repeat himself.

"Oh, yes, the sun!" Sebastian turned to face his brother while softly laying his face on the pillow. He thought for a while, as his brother watched.

"So?" Asked Santiago.

"Wait a second, I am thinking." Replied Sebastian. He began to remember where he had been before, and thought about Spain and the classes he had been learning in geography that year in school.

"The sun appeared in Spain the next day. It materialized from behind a wall of carved wooden fans that could have only come from Valencia, you know like the one mom uses at church. The fans moved naturally, as if a hand was shifting them gently back and forth. They stirred the visible heat waves created by the sunlight, which in turn generated more waves that could be seen miles away. Then, mimicking the clouds, the fans started to close down and disappear one by one, from right to left, allowing the sun to be fully visible. The color of the sun was golden yellow like on the Spanish flag, brilliant and captivating. It felt like an illusion the way the sun shined in Spain that morning."

All the while, Santiago felt himself transported into this world he had never seen or heard of.

"As the sun came through the fans, it shined over the highway of Cantabria in the northern coast of Spain, near the little town of Villahormes. The road was quiet. Nothing could be heard for miles, just the sound of a gentle breeze and the crashing rhythms of ocean waves exploding to the north, echoing in the distance like the beating claps of Asturian flamenco. The day was picture perfect as the light from the sun reflected on the sandy earth like a mirror toward the sky, fracturing the light into a million directions. The air was cool and crisp.

A little passenger bus came into view on the highway and it slowed down toward a sign that read *'Beach Stop'*. So, a woman and two children got off the little red bus. Standing on the sidewalk outside the bus door, the woman turned around to ask the driver how late the bus service would run. The kids ran off toward a dirt path, framed by bright green grasses and weeds. The woman hollered at the children to wait for her as she finished her conversation with the bus driver. The bus door closed and the woman in the blue and yellow cotton dress waved goodbye and turned around to walk toward the path where the children were playing. The youngsters were about six years old and appeared very similar to each other, with the exception that one was a boy and the other, a girl."

Sebastian unexpectedly climbed up on his bed and pointed to the sun collage on the wall and said with a deeper voice, mimicking the TV commercial announcer they often made fun of, "The sun was shining bright as some small round clouds moved along inland pushed by the strength of the ocean breeze. It was shining high but then low. The sun would slowly move up in the sky and down toward the earth like your bouncing basketball when you play in the garage downstairs. In *sllowwwww motionnnnn, uppp and downnn*."

Sebastian giggled. It was like a different person inside of him, Santiago thought.

Sebastian sat down back on his bed and extended his hands as he said, "The mother, seeing the bouncing sun in the sky along the sea, became very frightened and extended her hands out to call her children back to her. She was still a couple of steps behind them, for she could not match the energy of her little creatures. She finally got a hold of the girl and held her hand as all three stopped abruptly when they felt the heat of the sun reach them closely in one of the sun bounces. The earth moved, like that earthquake rattle we felt at Christmas time last year. Remember when the Christmas tree fell down all over our gifts? The woman knelt down to protect her daughter, who was by now weeping from the sudden movement below her feet. The boy ran back to his mother and grabbed on to her leg with his head secured under her arm. They all stood still while the sun bounced once more very high into the sky and finally came back down, punching against the earth so powerfully that it created a sinkhole in the ground. It was almost as if it wanted to tunnel a hole through to the other side of the planet. From the pressure forced into the ground, the mother and children were thrown like cloth dolls backwards toward a grassy field and landed on their backs about twenty feet behind them. The sun then went up again into the sky high above them and slowly stopped bouncing altogether. The supernatural event left a fair amount of dust and a confusing gale in the region. As it started to subside, the woman and the two children stood up, all coated with dust on their clothes and exposed skin. The lady looked at her children to see if they were alright and noticed a strong tan line forced on their skin from the power of the light. She then looked at her arms and noticed the same. They looked around and as the dust settled, they saw the sinkhole that the sun had formed around a rocky area closest to the sea. The sun's heat had created a patch of what appeared to be creamy colored sand. The family walked slowly toward the gaping hole. It was mesmerizing and beautiful, like a mirage."

Santiago's bright green eyes opened wide as if he were part of the story.

"The little boy couldn't believe it, and rubbed his eyes to check if what he was seeing was real. The light of the sun started to reflect on the sand that the sun had left off on that patch of ground. After a moment passed, they felt safe enough to walk toward the sinkhole. Rocks appeared to have been pushed back from the impact and intense power of the sun as it punched into the earth. They approached the sandy area with caution. The kids separated from their mother and walked around the shell-shaped platform. The mother was completely quiet, still in shock that she had been present to a miracle, looking around to see if anyone else had been witness to such an inexplicable phenomenon. She sat down on the sand bank and sank both her bronzed fingers into it as she felt the heat of the sun still emanating from within the dune. She looked to both sides and saw her children running now more comfortably on the sand. Then, she laid down on her back and looked up to observe the sun covering her eyes from the brilliant light. It was still there, high above her in the sky, no longer bouncing.

The kids played on the sand and after a while, they heard a strange noise in the distance. It sounded like when the water is turned off and the pipes get full of air when turned back on. They could also hear the waves from the sea pounding the coast many meters away. The sound of the air pipes became stronger. Deep in the sinkhole toward the rocky area in the back, they gradually saw water spreading from under the sand and rocks. It was as if the ocean water was being pumped slowly into the sinkhole. The woman yelled for her children to come to her, unsure of what would happen next. They obeyed and sat next to her as they all watched how water slowly filled in the sinkhole to create a perfect shell-shaped beach. The water reached up to their feet and then receded, gentler than ocean waves. It was like the sun had known what it was doing."

"Wow!" It was the only thing Santiago could say as they heard intense laughter coming from outside the door of their room. Their parents' friends were still visiting and now appeared to be inebriated. Sebastian stayed quiet for a while just listening to the noise coming from the living room. He then laid back down on the bed. He covered himself and looked up at the space of the ceiling he was so accustomed to visiting every night. Santiago asked his brother about the father of the kids in the story.

"Their father left them." Sebastian just blurted it out, not even thinking for a second.

Santiago then asked, in search of a happy ending, "And what happened next at the sinkhole?"

Sebastian responded that they stayed there at the beach and the children played on the water for hours until it was time to leave.

"By the late afternoon, the woman packed up while the children dried themselves with their towels. They left the sinkhole and began walking, the woman looking back at the sinkhole beach to see if it was still there. The children followed her toward the highway just a short walk away, all the while, the sun shined down on them. After about six that evening, the sun started to pull further away from the land toward the west. The children could see their long shadows on the right side of their bodies as they crossed the highway over to the little neighborhood of Villahormes. The highway was quiet and empty of any traffic just as it was earlier that morning. While crossing the highway, they heard church bells in the distance, and the woman and her children followed the sound for a couple of blocks. After a long, straight, one-way road lined with tall Italian cypresses, they reached a big white house that stood two stories high next to a little dilapidated chapel. The children looked up and saw a sign and above it two bells on the tower, releasing the distinct sound they had heard as they crossed the highway. The bells stopped as the front doors of the little chapel opened and an old man dressed completely in black appeared. Beautiful choral music could be heard coming from inside the chapel."

All the while Sebastian had been looking up into the ceiling of his bedroom not realizing that his brother had already fallen asleep, as he continued telling his story.

"The man greeted the family with a warm handshake and kind words. No one could hear them because the choir music drowned their voices. The man made a motion welcoming the family into the chapel. The sound of the music increased as they entered deeper into the little dark space." Sebastian then stopped and yawned heavily stretching as much as he could.

"Inside, past the door, the children discovered a three tier sparkling chandelier. Toward the end of the room was a wall decorated with a lifelike painting of a wooded area, and in front of it was a life-size wooden sculpture of Jesus Christ on the cross. The choral music kept coming from above them but they could not see the singers. As they walked to the center of the chapel, the music quieted down and the woman was finally able to speak to the priest. She explained the details of the phenomena that had transpired earlier on their way to the beach as she shed fearful tears."

Sebastian turned toward his brother who was clutching his favorite old Topo Gigio doll and eyes closed.

"Santiago!" Exclaimed Sebastian. He called on him again but his brother didn't respond. Sebastian yawned once more.

"I've been telling you about these people and you're asleep? Santiago!"

Santiago, feeling disturbed, turned sideways away from his brother and responded with a grunting sound. Sebastian took a huge sigh and closed his eyes for a moment. Wanting to end the story that had now taken him far away from his reality, he looked up at the ceiling and waited for the clouds to come back. Sebastian continued to hear the voices of his parents and their friends outside in the living room. The sounds of the voices quickly transformed in the darkness of the bedroom becoming ghostly and distant. He could in fact see the rhythm of the tones reverberate on the ceiling of the room like the curvilinear shapes of sound waves. The clouds followed soon after. The waves of sound appeared over the clouds and released rays of light like the corona mass ejections on the surface of the sun. The light radiating from the ceiling was bluish green and at times bright red and purple. The waves created by the voices would sometimes disappear below the swirling gray clouds. And the sound of laughter reacted differently in the clouds. Laughter would release sudden lightning-like rays of light. The white light was so bright that it prevented Sebastian from looking at it directly. The sounds dissipated slowly as time progressed, then the room went quiet, like the chapel in his story. He then, feeling completely fatigued, fell asleep.

Both brothers disliked Sundays. It meant getting up very early, dressing up in scratchy constricting clothes, and going to church. But when they woke up that morning, they saw that it was raining and felt a bit of hope that they may not have to go. They both looked at their father in disbelief when he told them that they were still going.

"Do we really have to go? It's raining." Said Santiago as if their parents were unaware of the weather outside.

"Yes, we do." Responded Michelle, pushing them to go to their bedroom. Santiago ran over to his mother and while hugging her said, "I don't want to go, I love you."

To which she responded, "I love you too deary, but that's not going to work, go get ready!"

Sebastian, Santiago, and Camilla, their 10-year old cousin, sat together four rows from the front of the church altar and whispered all throughout the service. They could see the priest perspiring just as bad as Esteban. The heat and humidity in the church was so thick, Sebastian was able to write his name on the pew in front of him. They didn't pay any attention to the proceedings. Camilla's mother who was Esteban's sister, was sitting next to Michelle, and Esteban was in the center of the pew. They all stood up then knelt, then stood up again, all the while the kids gossiped about the people in the church. Santiago pointed to the altar boys standing on the pulpit, also disconnected from their service responsibilities. Michelle sometimes looked down the pew over to the kids and made stern faces to make them pay attention, while Camilla's mother, Justine, stood with both of her arms up listening to the priest's every word. Then the priest started a chant and Justine followed his lead, then by the rest of the congregation. By now, the rain had subsided and the sun peeked through some gray and white clouds.

After the service, the family all stood outside the church waiting for Michelle and Justine to return from using the   restroom. On the way to the car, Sebastian leaned over to Santiago and quietly told him that aunt Justine's underwear was showing over her blouse and she looked ridiculous. Santiago chuckled out loud, then called his mom's attention by pointing at Justine's behind.

Michelle smiled politely and walked out quickly in front of them to avoid having to see her kids making fun of their aunt. Looking inside the church at the remaining parishioners, Camilla was oblivious to her cousin's antics. Poor Justine had been the joke of everyone in the family for years because of her odd personality. As her daughter, Camilla had no choice but to put up with her. Sebastian and Santiago thought aunt Justine was quite entertaining. The same went for their mother, who had to live under the same roof with silly Justine when she first married Esteban because his parents were still exerting control over their adult son.

Every Sunday after church service, everyone gathered at a different family member's home where they ordered lunch from a nearby Chinese restaurant and enjoyed each other's company while exchanging the latest gossip. That afternoon, it happened to take place at Esteban and Michelle's apartment. Aunt Justine and Camilla were there. While the adults sat in the living room that faced the front of the apartment, the children were all in the balcony playing board games and having a good time watching the cars drive by the road in front of the apartment building.

After everyone had finished lunch, the kids heard a car park in front of the building and some ruckus coming from downstairs. The three kids simultaneously rested their heads on the metal railing looking down to see what was occurring below. Santiago recognized a distant female voice first and screamed out. "Granny! Is that Granny?"

Asking his brother for confirmation, Sebastian turned to look at Santiago and then looked down again to see if he could make out the face of the woman getting out of the car.

"Yes, I think it's Granny." Camilla smiled as if it was her own grandmother that had come to visit.

When Michelle, Esteban, and Justine heard Santiago's excitement, they got up and Michelle asked Santiago what was happening.

"Granny came to visit! She's downstairs!" He hadn't even finished before he was racing out the front door and down the three flights of stairs to the sidewalk below. Sebastian and Camilla stayed in the balcony waving and throwing air kisses at Sebastian's grandmother, Blanche.

She was beautiful just like Michelle, with long dark hair pulled back in a knot on the top of her head and an elegant pearl broach that she always wore when she visited her grandchildren. She was wearing a suit that could have been made by a famous fashion designer, yet she sewed it herself. Everyone in the apartment was now in the balcony looking down and waving at Blanche, while Michelle shouted to her mother to let her know that Santiago was on his way to greet her. Blanche waited next to the car as the taxi driver unloaded her bags.

Blanche was as affectionate as Santiago. As soon as she saw Sebastian on the balcony she began to shout. "Treassuurrrred beauties of granny!" She repeated.

"I am on my way up there!" She continued.

By then, Santiago had reached the lobby of the building. He opened the metal front door, jumped off the three steps in front of the entrance, and took a quick step past the front walkway.

Michelle, observing the action from above, screamed at the top of her lungs, "STOP SAN, DO NOT CROSS THE STREET!"

Santiago ran across the street without looking, only fixated on reaching his grandmother. He didn't know there was a car coming down the street toward him, narrowly missing him.

Blanche dropped the bag that the taxi driver had just given her and ran over to catch Santiago who was frozen on the street, petrified from the incident. The driver that

Santiago had crossed in front of got out of his car and rushed over to see if he was all right. Michelle had arrived downstairs as if by magic, and knelt down to embrace both her mother and Santiago who were still on the street clutching each other. Poor Blanche was crying and shaking. Blanche then got up and looked up at the rest of the family and other neighbors from the building that had come out to their balconies, curious about the commotion on the street. She made a sign to Esteban motioning that everything was fine. He ran out of the door and down the stairs to see for himself. Downstairs, Michelle cried along with her mother as she grasped her child who appeared to be shocked from the incident and all the subsequent attention. The taxi and the other car left minutes after, then Blanche, Michelle, and Santiago walked upstairs to the apartment.

On the way up to the apartment, Blanche and Michelle framed Santiago's body as each one held one of his hands. Blanche started her famous chant again, "Treassurrred beauty of granny! Treassurrred beauty of granny! I brought you and your brother some special gifts." This was enough for Santiago to smile again and get his happy-go-lucky personality back.

Esteban met them half way down the stairs and walked

back up with them. Once upstairs, everyone greeted Blanche. Justine, kneeling down to Santiago's level, hugged him tenderly, making the sign of the cross on his forehead. He just stood there looking down, not returning the hug. Santiago was still shocked. It seemed the event had taken a lot of energy out of him. Sebastian and Michelle were also in shock while Esteban held his son and spoke to him in a serious voice. "Never do that again, you hear me?"

Santiago looked down again and ran into his room completely embarrassed. Both Sebastian and Camilla followed Santiago into the room and closed the door behind them. Michelle was so shaken that her husband held her for a couple of minutes as she wept. Blanche, who by now had stopped sobbing, caressed her daughter's head and told her that nothing had happened, it was just a scare.

The event involving Santiago fast-forwarded the day into the dark hours. Aunt Justine and Camilla had already gone home but the kids could still hear the voice of their adored grandmother coming from outside their bedroom door. They could hear both their mother and Blanche chitchatting about Esteban, so the children assumed that their dad wasn't close by.

That Sunday, the kids were in bed by eight. Their school uniforms were hung in an organized fashion from the knobs of their closet doors. Their school bags held all their Monday assignments, notebooks, and schoolbooks. Santiago appeared relaxed in his bed as Sebastian checked the clock to confirm that the alarm had been set for the following morning.

In their nightgowns, both Blanche and Michelle walked in their bedroom. Neither had makeup on, which Sebastian found odd since he had never seen his grandmother without it. They sat between the beds to be close to both kids and gave each a hug and a kiss before asking them to pray. Today's prayer was different; Blanche discussed Santiago's incident earlier that day and thanked God for saving his life. Michelle followed with an "Amen!" Then they all recited a bedtime prayer.

Santiago asked his mom, "Where's dad?" She smiled at him as she often did. Blanche extended her hand to grab her daughter's hand.

"He's in the bedroom, he'll come back later to check on you boys." She replied.

Sebastian smiled at his mother in his usual loving way.

The room turned dark; only a reflection from the bright sheets showed both boys laying straight down the center of their respective beds. The air was radiant this evening; it was a cool breeze that felt colder as it moved through the oscillating fan in the room. Both boys were unusually quiet, as if neither one of them wanted to bring up the conversation about Santiago's close call. Sebastian rubbed his eyes a little and his ceiling visions returned. Oblivious to the drama above, Santiago was already being seduced by sleep. Sebastian was dazed by the light from the fireworks show above him, yet at his age he couldn't comprehend the meaning behind this apparition. Sebastian began to see sparks of bright white light fall from the ceiling into the room, something that he had never seen before. He turned to follow one of the sparks, which fell around him like droplets of water, surrounding his bed and filling the room in a blanket of lights. Then the sparks came down more pronounced and in more quantity. Sebastian became petrified and raised his head and chest to examine what was happening. It was like a meteor shower had hit the room. The sparks just hit and expanded across the surfaces and then disappeared without explanation. Sebastian kept looking around the room and then turned to look over at Santiago's bed to see if he was okay. Unexpectedly, a spark fell on Sebastian's head and he saw the light splash all over the proximity of his body like an exploding balloon full of fire, yet he didn't feel heat or burn from it. Not having felt any pain from the light show, Sebastian felt more at ease and laid back down on the bed. He kept looking at the spinning clouds above him and the sparks slowly subsided.

The Sun Night

Have you ever seen the sun come out at night? My brother and I used to fantasize about things like that. We could see the moon out during the day at times, why not the sun at night?

The last week of school was over and the kids were excited about their upcoming trip. Grandmother Blanche had stayed with the family the whole week and would also be going to the beach with them. The kids didn't ask many questions, but were always listening to the adult conversations to find out what was happening since Michelle and Esteban were not very forthcoming with details. On the way home from school on the last Friday before vacation, Sebastian and Santiago both asked their mother about the trip. In the past, their parents would often invite friends of theirs to stay at the beach house their family owned in Santa Clara, about two hours away from the city.

"Will cousin Camilla and aunt Justine come to the beach too?" Sebastian asked.

"I don't know." His mother shrugged.

"We've asked aunt Justine if she could come but as you know she doesn't drive at night."

The kids giggled as they often did when they thought of aunt Justine.

"We wanted to see Camilla again." Sulked Santiago, disappointed that she might not be able to make it.

"Well, don't feel defeated Santiago, she may still come, we just have to make sure she travels during the daytime. Her eyesight is not that good. I have to do grocery shopping for the trip, so I am going to drop you off by the house and leave you with Granny while I do the shopping, okay?"

They didn't answer. Santiago in particular loved to go shopping at the supermarket. The toy isle was his favorite, of course.

"I want to go!" He said out loud, and then repeated himself a couple more times, before she stopped him in mid-sentence.

"Sebastian, do you want to go too?" And thinking of the toy isle as well, he smiled and only answered with an affirmative shake of his head that Michelle could see through the reflection of her VW's rear view mirror.

At the supermarket, they went about their business getting meat, bread, butter, milk, and much more for their beach month-long vacation. Once they were getting ready to leave the store, they saw a flash of light coming from outside through the store windows. They all looked up and felt the jolt that followed, which shook the whole building and the shoppers inside. Large drops of water hit the pavement as shoppers ran into the store in an effort to avoid the storm that was approaching with alarming speed. Michelle and the kids were unprepared for the ensuing thunderstorm so they waited inside the store past the registers, but the area began to get full from other shoppers with the same idea. Santiago and Sebastian observed a couple running and covering their heads with newspapers, but by the time they got to their vehicles, they were completely soaked. The brothers both looked at each other and laughed at the absurdity of the situation. Michelle, who was chatting with another lady waiting in the same area, noticed what happened and gave them a disapproving look. The rain kept coming down hard, and the parking lot started to flood. Sebastian spotted the sun peek out from behind one of the clouds as they relocated to a covered area outside of the store. It looked as though the worst of the storm had passed. Moments later, the rain subsided and everyone that was waiting to leave the store ran toward their vehicles. The kids' feet got completely drenched from the large puddles of water they had to go through to get to the car.

Once in the VW, Michelle moved all the groceries into the back seat and asked the boys to sit on the front seat while she took the cart back to the store. When she returned, she asked the kids to take their shoes and socks off, while pulling paper towel squares from the glove compartment so that they could dry their feet. With an exhausted sigh, Michelle pulled out of the parking lot.

That night, there was no sign of Esteban. Like a broken

record, the elements of his absence were apparent. Michelle was conflicted and blamed herself for his ways and lack of presence in the home, especially for dinner time when he could be spending time with the boys. That evening was just like any other Friday; Sebastian and Santiago ate grilled cheese sandwiches along with an untouched salad that Michelle had to force them to finish. Michelle sat pensively next to Blanche, while the boys wondered what their mother could be thinking of. Michelle just sat there without any reaction while Blanche's mouth moved without stopping for a breath. Michelle looked far past Santiago's head toward the living room, then further away, past the buildings outside, and the sky behind them.

In bed that night, the air felt chilly and damp unlike other nights from the past, a gift from the earlier storm. The children were in their beds, already tucked in and tired from all they had learned that school year, but relieved that they had a summer at the beach to look forward to. The room was quiet, and the only noise that could be heard was the oscillating fan moving from one side to the other.

"I had a dream last night and I tried to remember it all day. I was going to tell you on the way home from school but I forgot." Sebastian loved to talk about dreams and attentively asked his brother, "Yes, tell me, what did you dream about?"

He turned to face his brother in the dark. "Sebastian, I dreamed that I was in a garage, with you and mom."

Sebastian responded, "Yes?"

Santiago proceeded, "We were walking in the garage to get to our car and then we heard a loud noise, but not like the thunder we heard today. It was more like the growl of a tiger, but bigger! Then we saw a man and a woman running and hiding behind a car but it was weird because we could see three levels of the garage at once as if there were no walls holding the garage levels together. Then out of nowhere we all found out where the growl was coming from. It was a huge T-Rex as tall as two stories. The dinosaur was so big it kept hitting the ceiling above with his head while pieces of concrete fell on it and the cars in its vicinity. The T-Rex followed the couple that hid behind the car and once it approached them, we saw the people run behind a big wall of concrete. The dinosaur was furious because he couldn't catch the people; he was hungry, you know."

His brother replied, "What a strange dream, Santiago!"

"He was enraged and growled some more and this caused the garage structure to shake as if it was the epicenter of an earthquake." Santiago mimicked the sounds the dinosaur may have made.

"You and mom started to scream when you saw me under a car, but then I woke up, I think, I can't remember anything else. I don't know what happened to you, mom, the people in the garage, or the T-Rex."

There was quiet in the room for a little while.

"I wonder what a dinosaur was doing inside of a parking garage, that's just weird! No?" Asked Santiago.

"What I want to know is what were you doing under the car?" Asked Sebastian.

"I don't know, maybe I was trying to hide away from the T-Rex."

After a couple of minutes of silence, Santiago asked his brother, "What is the first thing you want to do when we get to Santa Clara?"

Sebastian replied, "I'd love to go to the beach and then take a nap in the hammocks. I hope Camilla can come too so we can play. It's not as much fun when she's not there."

Santiago agreed.

They'd known for some time that Camilla's mom, aunt Justine, wasn't doing well, and she couldn't drive anymore because of her vision problems. Perhaps someone else could take Camilla and aunt Justine to the beach, they would just have to wait to find out.

A little after midnight, the door of their bedroom

opened quietly. The room was dark and not even a face or expression could be seen on the body that had entered the room, only the brightness of a white guayabera shirt. Esteban was still wearing his work clothes. He walked in the room as if expecting the children to be awake, only to see their resting little bodies in their beds. He could make out the silhouette of his boys from the light that always came in the room at night. They were both in a deep sleep. Their dad walked slowly to the row of windows and stood there looking out for a couple of minutes, appearing to admire the view. Most homes were dark, with a couple of dim lights in the distance. He continued to stare absentmindedly out into the distance. Esteban then turned and looked at his kids as a sudden cool breeze rushed into the room and made his dark hair move in all directions. The movement of his hair created an electrical spark that he felt travel from the tip of the hair to his scalp. At the same time, he saw the spark of light reflect on the window glass. He pushed himself back from the jolt of the electrical charge, tip toed swiftly toward the door, opening and shutting it closed in an instant.

Neither child heard or felt anything as they were in their slumber dreaming away about the sun and their upcoming trip to the beach.

In the darkness of night, moaning and voices were heard in the distance coming from outside the room but the children heard nothing, as they were fully immersed in their imagining. Then the voices turned into screams and blurs of loud words. If the boys were awake, they would have seen the shape of two figures: a man sitting on the side of the bed, flapping his arms and slurring his words in the direction of a female standing on the opposite side of the room. They would have seen the man throw his glass, with remnants of alcohol in the direction of the standing female, missing her by a foot. He stood up and stormed out of the room. The woman resisted following her husband, locking the door and screaming horrifically. Her husband returned to the hallway and screamed dreadful things back at her through the locked door. He then turned around and was surprised to see his youngest son, Santiago, framed by the doorway of his kids' bedroom looking out and asking his dad what had gone wrong. Santiago stood there shaking. Behind him and behind the door, was Sebastian crying quietly while he held his right fist in his mouth to prevent himself from making any loud noise. Their father didn't know what to do, so he also yelled at his children to get back in their room and their beds.

"Get the hell back in your room, you should be asleep!"

Sebastian's arm reached out to grab Santiago from behind the door and pulled him into their room, quickly locking the door. From the thrust of the pull, they both fell back onto Santiago's bed.

They both trembled from the clatter and cuddled each other. Everything went quiet after the kids went back in the room, with the exception of a door slamming. The kids held each other, Sebastian caressing Santiago's hair softly and ensuring that everything was going to be all right. And then to distract him, Sebastian continued telling his brother about the sun.

"The night was quiet with a light breeze moving over the warm water of the ocean. There were hardly any waves on the dark sea, only a glassy reflection on the surface. Flying fish jumped out of the water curious to see the magnificent views. They created small splashes on the water before diving back into the sea. Then waves began to form as if the water was shaken scared. Prickly ripples formed everywhere around an island causing water to grow as tall as hills and emptying into the vast ocean away from it. The hot magma bubbled up from the pressure of all the gases at the mouth of the volcano in this island in the middle of the vast ocean. It exploded, causing globs of molten rock to jump in the sea, splashing everywhere in precise patterns designed by the wrath of nature. The intense heat of the lava created a bright orange and red halo everywhere around the volcano that could be seen miles away like search lights moving in different directions. The evaporation of sea water as the lava made contact created smoke screens that blurred the environment like Japanese rice paper panels appearing and disappearing from one moment to the next.

On the other side of the island, Koa and Hana lived with their children, Elio and his younger sister Aolani. Their exposed skin was dark and they dressed with leaves found in the flora of the island. They appeared to have finished eating their supper when the earth started to shake faintly under their feet. They heard rumbling noises coming from the north side of the island where the volcano was located. It sounded like thunder under the ground traveling to reach the islanders. Aolani, who was cleaning inside of a shack, ran outside upon first hearing the sound and grabbed onto Elio's arm. He figured out the sound was coming from the mount of light. While covering his sister's eyes, Koa and Hana gathered next to the children on either side as they viewed brilliant lights amidst the darkness of night. Aolani shaking just like the earth below her began to scream out loud, 'Here it comes, here it comes.' The intense light shot straight upward into the sky as if trying to touch the clouds above. The earth continued to shake while they tried to hold onto each other. Koa looked around to ensure everyone's safety. The mount continued to spew magma upward and in all directions with a thick white smoke that further lit the sky as if it was daytime erasing the light of the shining stars completely.

Then the rumbling sound vanished abruptly and everything went quiet. They all looked at each other and without saying a word, knelt to the floor and placed the palms of their hands facing down to feel the earth below them. Nothing moved. Suddenly, a flock of sea birds scared them as they fluttered off quickly, scared off by something ominous. Hana's sensitive hand felt the earth fragments below her begin to jump and shake again. The rumbling returned ten times stronger. The family was knocked off of their place. Aolani jumped and began to sing again, 'Here is comes, here it comes.' They kept on looking up at the mount after they sensed a much deeper deafening uproar of impending total destruction. They heard a huge thunk sound and looked up at once to witness a huge sphere of fire releasing slowly from beneath the earth through the mouth of the volcano, and out toward the sky. The light of the fireball was so intense, they all had to look away and cover their faces with palm fronds. They could feel the heat of the sun very close to them. And the earth continued to shake causing cracks on the ground.

In the distance, they witnessed huge masses of earth rippling, swallowing everything with it. Coconuts, leaves, and other fruits fell off trees everywhere while cracks began to appear on the ground all around them. The islanders wondered if they were secured in this patch of land close to the beach. The giant fire ball kept moving up slowly into the sky above the mouth of the volcano creating strong shadows in all directions. The sky became bright as day and the sun grew larger as it moved further up into the higher atmosphere. Cascades of molten rock drained off its sides back toward the earth creating small hills everywhere they touched down."

Santiago asked his brother, "Wow, Sebastian! What happened to those people?"

Sebastian replied, "They were fine. Once the quake subsided, Koa stood up contemplating the mountain of fire in complete bewilderment. A moment later out of his mouth came a soft chant saluting the sun of night present in front of them. His family followed by waving to welcome the sun. Koa's melody echoed in the valley toward the volcano and all around the island until it reached the sea. Hearing the cheerful sounds, the flying fish returned to happily splash."

Sebastian closed his eyes and waited a while as Santiago just looked up at the ceiling of his room imagining what those islanders would have gone through. Sebastian then turned to look at his brother and asked him if he was excited about their trip to the beach, to which he responded with a positive manner.

Santiago then out of nowhere asked, "What is going to happen to our parents?"

His concerned brother responded, "I wish I knew."

In the darkness of the night and the coolness of the air, the children kept quiet just holding each other, then finally falling asleep.

In the morning, each child was in his own bed. A light knock on the door of their bedroom woke them up in a snap. Santiago turned to look up toward his brother's bed and both looked at each other as if communicating mentally that everything was all right as Sebastian had promised the night before. Santiago got out of his bed, unlocked the door, and turned the doorknob slowly. He looked up and the comforting figure of his mother appeared behind the door. She walked in and laid down next to Santiago on his bed. Sebastian sat on his bed with pajamas soaked with sweat from the heat of the summery morning. Michelle had heard Santiago ask his father about the fight they had the night before. She looked at them, then looked down troubled, confused, and embarrassed.

Her face was one of those that could tell stories. The bags under her eyes said it all. She spoke to them in the quiet motherly way she often did when she wanted to express her affection toward them.

"Your dad and I had a very bad fight last night, and I am so sorry that you had to hear it."

Her eyes watered and tears traveled down both of her cheeks. Santiago quickly went over to hug her, almost pushing her to the floor.

"We love you, mommy." He said. Sebastian followed his brother's action.

He looked at her and said, "Yes, we love you very much, mommy." Michelle explained to her kids in the simplest form possible about her problems with their dad. He was drinking too much and didn't know when to stop. The children could now understand why their mom always looked so anxious when their dad was not around. But in some way, they always knew. They knew because they also missed their dad at home. They missed him playing with them as he used to when they were younger. They missed him taking them to fly kites and playing ball.

Then out of nowhere, Santiago asked his mother, "Are you and dad going to get a divorced?"

She quickly smiled, clearing the tears off her face, "No San, it's just a fight. Everyone fights; you two fight all the time. Everyone has a difference of opinion at times, that doesn't mean we have to get divorced. And how do you know what that word means? Huh?"

She rapidly got up and asked her kids to get ready, and started pulling the sheets off their beds to get them washed. By then, Blanche had walked in the room dressed up and wished everyone a happy morning. Michelle and the children acted as if nothing had happened. Blanche hadn't heard the commotion of the night before but knew something was not right in the house.

She followed her daughter into the bathroom where she stood waiting for the water in the shower to turn warm for her children's bath.

Blanche asked, "Where is Esteban?"

Michelle didn't respond.

Blanche asked again, with a more concerned tone.

After a moment, Michelle responded quietly so that her children wouldn't hear, "I'll tell you in a moment."

While the children were in the bathroom, Michelle proceeded to tell her mother all about the fight and how the children were awakened by it. Michelle expressed her regret that the kids had to hear them fight so often. She knew they could hear them fight.

Blanche, who had never married after her second husband died, was very vocal about her daughter's choice for a husband and this was a perfect opportunity to make a point of it.

"You see? I told you that man was going to make your life miserable."

Michelle answered defensively, "He's not a bad person, we just have too many fights."

Blanche continued, "He drinks too much. Do you know where he goes to drink all the time?"

Michelle responded in a dry judgmental fashion, "Yes, mother." She became uncomfortable having to explain details with her mother and quickly changed the subject.

"I hear Santiago. Let's talk about this later." She walked away toward the hallway to her children's bedroom to go get them ready.

Mid-morning, Blanche took her daughter and grandchildren to breakfast at a nearby café. When they returned to the apartment, Esteban was home. He greeted everyone as if nothing had ever happened, and Michelle followed suit. Blanche acted as if she knew nothing but still with a special twinkle in her eye. She wasn't scared of him. She asked him questions to make him uncomfortable, acting as if nothing had ever happened the night before.

Santa Clara of the Heavens

School vacation was a path to new adventures. Our family vacations to the beach were the best times my brother and I ever had together. We didn't know of anything better. Apparently, the road on the beach sand doesn't exist. Did I dream that we drove in the car through a road on the beach or is it a memory from a previous or future life?

The journey to the beach was as fun as its final destination. The trip began early the next morning. Esteban, Michelle, the kids, and Blanche all fit cozily inside the packed VW. The trip was two hours long, which for the kids felt much more like a whole day journey. Salsa music could be heard from the radio as the family all looked out into the vistas on the road to Santa Clara, the beach where Esteban's family owned a vacation home. Past the sleeping Indian mountain could be seen the most beautiful views the children had ever experienced. Almost an hour into the trip was where the first stop always occurred, up the mountain where cars could park to take in breathtaking views of the land below. Esteban parked the VW Bug as close to the precipice as possible, which Michelle always found terrifying. She held her breath and grabbed onto her door handle as her husband slowed into an available parking spot. Once he turned off the ignition and pulled the parking lever, she took a big breath as the children watched the view in awe in front of them from the back seat. Their parents opened the door and Michelle let the children out by pulling her seat forward. Sebastian and Santiago jumped out of the car as quickly as they could, stepping over their grandmother who stayed behind.

"Don't you want to come out for a moment, Mom?"

Asked Michelle.

"No dear, I'll just stay in. I'm scared of heights and I've seen that landscape more times than I can remember."

Outside the car, Esteban sat on the hood as he looked out into the distance. The kids followed suit, Santiago standing as close to the cliff as the signs allowed.

Michelle screamed at him, "Come back here, you are going to fall and get killed."

He followed instructions repentantly. Michelle grabbed a couple of drinks from a cooler she had prepared for the trip and handed them to the boys. Esteban asked her if he could have one and so she passed one to him as well. He took it but didn't thank her, just continued looking away.

Fifteen minutes had passed when Blanche shouted out from inside the car, "It's time to go, or we're going to hit traffic." She knew better.

Summertime drew many people to the beaches and traffic would often get much worse if they were caught on the road any later.

As they left the city and drove closer into the provincial towns near the beaches, a certain peace could be felt in the air. The flora got thicker and greener, and the man-made structures became less modern and more appropriate for the smaller towns they passed along the main road.

An hour and a half into their journey in the back of the VW, Blanche spoke to her daughter and son-in-law while the children napped on either side of her, further accentuating her attractive curves.

The VW rushed through the road down to Santa Clara as fast as it could while its passengers looked out at little towns pass by on the left and right.

Nearing the beach, the traffic seemed to disappear entirely. But the trip wasn't over until they crossed the beach road. It was a strip of road that was only accessible on low tide and the only way to cross into the beach area of Santa Clara.

Esteban woke the kids from their road nap. This was a spot that the children could not miss. The idea of driving on a road that was submerged under water part of the time was just thrilling. As soon as they got up, they both yawned and looked out of their windows to see where they were and noticed a patch of palm trees and a sign that read *'Beach Road – Next 1 mile.'*

"We're almost there, Santiago." Exclaimed Sebastian.

Blanche grabbed both kids and squeezed as hard as she could. When Santiago looked up at his grandmother, she noticed that his green eyes looked brighter than ever, perhaps from the abundance of sunshine.

Their dad was as excited as the kids and said out loud, "I'll try not to let the car sink into the ocean now," as he drove onto the beach road.

The first part of the road was just like driving on a regular concrete road, but as they drove closer to the water, there was more sand covering the surface. Sebastian in particular became worried about this as he could only imagine the worst. He was sitting on the side facing the open ocean and had prime view of the waves coming in toward the road, and toward the car. He became mesmerized by the waves and the ocean foam shapes left by the tires of the cars ahead of them. They resembled different types of shell shapes as they reflected from the light of the sun. Santiago was just thrilled about driving through the watery sand road as he could see the ocean waves forming rather closely but never reaching the road.

They continued on their way down this path and the road became more like driving in the sand. There were parts of the road that were just sand and water and sometimes cars got stuck. After about three quarters of the mile traveled on the sandy way, they encountered more pools of water and had to slow down in order to avoid splashing.

"Go faster, Daddy!" Santiago shouted as he expected to see some of the splash, but his father had to slow down almost to a complete stop when they encountered a pile of cars trying to pass through a section of the road that was deeper in water.

They finally reached the end of the beach road and got back on their way, now passing the Rio Hato naval base before reaching the entrance to the Santa Clara beach district. Two hours had now passed and their journey was nearing the end.

Once in the town, the quiet roads reminded them of Sundays in the city when everyone stayed home to rest from the arduous workweek. Both Sebastian and Santiago looked out the windows to locate the vacation home they would be staying in. Esteban's cousin, who lived in the United States, owned the house. Since he only used it once a year, Esteban took advantage of the accommodations while it was not being used.

They finally reached the entrance to the house and Esteban stopped to get the gate unlocked. There was a short drive into the house from the entrance, which was framed with beautiful bright purple and red bougainvillea.

The house was in front of them; a one-story ranch style home with an open cabana on the left side, and the main house on the right, both connected by a covered open area.

Esteban parked the car and the family got out as

quickly as they could, stretching in unison. There was a fresh welcoming breeze that moved through the space. Michelle and Blanche, with Esteban's assistance, took out all of the luggage and groceries from the VW's front compartment. The children explored the area outside of the cabana while their dad located the key in his pocket to open the front door. The house looked as if it had been unoccupied for some time, with spider webs in the corners of the window panes and dust everywhere. Once the door was unlocked, the adults disappeared inside, while Sebastian and Santiago found the open kitchen, a sort of grilling station between the cabana and the beach house. They were always impressed with the place. As they looked outside toward the front of the house, they remembered the flat open field properly manicured with trees lining the back end of the property. It was like a postcard, reflected Sebastian in his head, while all Santiago wanted to do was run around the cabana to discover what other secrets it kept.

"Santiago, Sebastian, come on over so you can see your room!" Exclaimed the female voice coming from the house.

Inside it smelled stale and musty. Michelle turned on the lights, dusted the dining room table, and checked over the open area of the living room.

In the kitchen, Esteban pulled the food out of bags into

the refrigerator he had just plugged onto the wall. Blanche disappeared into the restroom. The children ran into the living room where they found their mother.

"Where are we going to sleep, Mom?" Asked Santiago while discovering the living room space.

The house had two bedrooms. In order to fit everyone comfortably, she suggested that the kids sleep in the room with their grandmother since it had two queen size beds. They took their little bags and rushed into that bedroom, looked around at the accommodations, and quickly returned to the living room. There, they admired the nautical theme decorations that included navigation maps framed beautifully and placed thoughtfully on the walls near a large mid-century modern sofa bed. The walls were painted in a soft green that made the space feel like the inside of a yacht. Next to and above the sofa was a teak wood built-in bookcase that held picture books and knick-knacks of travels past. A large shell, a miniature boat carved in wood, and nautical flags filled the rest of the bookcase. On the very top, unreachable to the kids, was a beautiful detailed replica of the three-mast ship, the Santa Maria carved in wood. Sebastian walked over and quietly focused on each displayed item. When he reached the top, he noticed the Santa Maria.

He turned around and hollered at his mother, "Mom, can I play with the ship on the book case?" To which she quickly replied negatively.

"Those are for decoration my dear. Please don't touch anything." He turned around and kept looking mesmerized at the detail on the ship. The more he looked at it, the more the small details became visible to him; the little men on the deck, some of them climbing on the masts, even the cords that held the sails, and the cannons.

He then wondered about his brother's whereabouts.

Blanche walked out of the bathroom looking refreshed. The restroom was between the two bedrooms to one side of the house.

"Where is Santiago, Sebastian? He was just here." Asked Michelle.

His mother called, "Santiago?" He didn't answer. They looked all around the inside of the house but no sign of him, or his dad for that matter. Michelle, her mother, and Sebastian found them swinging peacefully out of two hammocks in the cabana building.

The cabana was quite quaint, with six large tree trunks that held the pointed roof covered in palm leaves stacked neatly and tightly. There were three classic wooden Adirondack chairs in the back of the cabana and two brightly colored cloth hammocks hung from three of the posts that faced the front.

"Wow, I see you've already started your vacation?" Inquired Michelle.

"This is the life." Replied her husband, followed by Santiago repeating his dad like an echo in a valley. Sebastian laughed and ran toward the hammock where his brother was, however Santiago continued to swing without regard. Michelle looked over and told her son to let his brother join him. He followed his mother's orders.

That afternoon, Sebastian and Santiago bugged their mother to let them go to the beach. Michelle preferred to go early in the mornings or later in the day to avoid the harsh sunshine, but after repeated requests, they were able to finally convince her to go even though it was much earlier. Michelle and the kids packed a beach bag, changed into their swim suits, and headed to the beach which was only a 10-minute walk. They walked down a narrow dirt road for about five minutes, and reached a paved opening between two beach houses with fifty-five steps that took them down to the beach level. They counted every step on the way down as their mother reminded them how far down the beach was from the top of the hill. As they got closer to the beach, they could hear the sound of the ocean waves crashing. Their bodies trembled with excitement. Michelle, who was a couple of steps behind them, could see their enthusiasm every time they looked back to see where she was. An unusual sweet smell filled the air. Past the steps was a straight path lined with tamarind trees. The children tried to jump up to catch some of the tamarind pods hanging off the trees but they couldn't reach. Michelle pulled down one of the branches to allow their children to grab a pod each, then they kept on walking down to the beach. As they broke into the pods and tasted the tart fruit, they continued following the path that turned into sand. The left side was lined with huge brightly flowering bougainvillea and on the right, was a little place they called the Swiss village because it housed several small vacation homes designed in a Swiss style with a pointed roof line and large windows that took in the views of the beach in front of the homes. There seemed to be people staying at some of the Swiss rentals as they noticed cars and beach ware by the sides of the chalets. They finally saw the path open up to welcome them to the yummy white soft sand and the ocean just a few short steps away. Both the children turned around to look for their mom. Behind her they could see all the steps they had just come down from. Once settled at the beach, Michelle kept reminding the children to be careful when getting in the water. And so they played among the waves and frolicked in the sand like children usually do. At this time of the day, most families had already left the beach, and only couples in love walked up and down the sun-kissed sand. Michelle felt fulfilled as she watched her kids trying to build a sand castle, then looked away past them to the vast ocean and the abrupt horizon line, wondering what was to be of her marriage and her life.

At about 5:30 p.m. the tide had almost reached the towels they had placed on the sand. Once Sebastian and Santiago were done building castles, they decided to take a walk to comb the beach for unusual shells. Their mother met them as they returned to go the other way. The beach was now completely empty except for them. As they walked near the line of waves crashing and receding, the kids had fun with their game of chasing and running from the waves. Along the way, they collected shells and carried as many as they could in their little hands. In one of those rolling waves, the three simultaneously saw a moving object in the water that was definitely not water, not sand, and definitely not shells.

Suddenly, Michelle screamed at the top of her lungs. "Santiago! Sebastian! Move away from the beach!"

They both threw all their collected shells toward the waves and ran faster than ever as they saw an ocean snake coming toward them. Sebastian got chills as he saw the undulating shape of the water snake move in and out. Since they didn't know what the snake would do, they ran away from the shoreline and toward their station on the sand, then quickly gathered their belongings and moved briskly away from the beach side.

"Are you okay, boys?" Asked Michelle, clearly worried about her kids. "We'll have to be more careful about getting into the ocean."

They walked back to the path that had brought them down to the beach originally to return to the vacation house. Sebastian just looked back at the waves to see where the snake had gone but it was hard to tell being so far from the shore. But he did see something else along the horizon. The sun was starting to touch the horizon line of the Pacific Ocean. He called out to his mother and brother to see this wonderful natural display. They all stopped and looked on as the sun moved behind just a few wispy clouds and slowly went down into the water.

"Can you hear the water burn, Santiago?" Sebastian exclaimed with excitement.

Santiago just smiled and nodded positively, showing

how thrilled he was.

They went up the fifty five steps, one at a time, taking a break here and there and looking up at what was left of the stairwell. Sebastian picked up bougainvillea flowers that had recently fallen on the sidewalk and one by one would give them to his mother. Michelle acted surprised every time and thanked him for the gesture.

Once at the beach house, their father had changed into his favorite pair of shorts and was swinging slowly from one of the hammocks in the cabana while Blanche sat in one of the comfy Adirondack chairs reading a book. There was a delightful smell of barbecue in the air that the children always associated with Santa Clara. They ran toward their dad as they approached the house and told him all about the sea snake. He expressed surprise and asked Michelle if there was anything to be worried about. The kids then went on to shower and change before supper.

They had their chicken barbecue dinner around a large round table outside in the cabana while Esteban watched his soccer game on the old bulky television set.

Nighttime had arrived and as Sebastian was getting ready for bed, he asked his mother if they could sleep in the living room so that they could finish watching a movie. Michelle didn't mind and allowed them to sleep on two sofa beds in the living room. She also thought that this would be best for her mother's privacy. Everyone went to bed early that night. There was a glow on Santiago and Sebastian's complexion from the afternoon of beach fun that reflected from the light of the television screen. They both laid on their stomachs as they watched the remaining 15 minutes of the animated movie they had started earlier that night. There was no other light except for a faint night-light on the wall in the hallway. Michelle and Blanche stopped by the living room before retiring to their rooms and wished the children a good night. Their dad, already inebriated, had fallen asleep earlier.

There was a light breeze that night, and the ceiling fan helped move the air towards the children below in their sofa beds. It was completely quiet, more so than their apartment in the city. They could hear their father snore all the way out into the living room. Santiago covered himself with the additional coverlet that their mother had brought from Blanche's room. Once the movie was over, Sebastian turned off the television and jumped into his sofa bed and made a comment about the place smelling weird.

"Raise the fan speed, that should help." Said Santiago. Sebastian followed his suggestion.

After a while, the children looked up and around the

room, trying to make up the different shapes from the new space they were sleeping in. Sebastian could see the silhouette of the galleon high on the book case, and the most colorful book spines jumped out more than others. Santiago could see a conch shell that looked formidably large from his point of view.

Out of the quiet, Santiago proclaimed "The sun today, it reminded me of the story you told me about the sun sinking into the ocean. It was so round and bright, and it even looked like there was a hotter fire coming from the outside of it, don't you think, Sebastian?"

His excitement grew. "It was brilliant! I had never seen the sun so big like that before. Why was it so big?"

Sebastian had no idea but still answered, "Maybe it's because we are closer to it here at the beach."

Sebastian, gazing at the ceiling, forced his eyes closed for a couple of seconds, then opened them again to reveal the never-ending vortex of gray clouds over him. It was quiet, darker, and mysterious in this distinctive house.

"What happened to the sun after it came out from inside the volcano, Sebastian?" Asked his brother, referring to the story he had heard the night before. Sebastian continued making the story up as he went.

"It went up in the sky over the ocean that night. The

flying sea birds all looked up at the sun and followed it by circling around it. Pretty soon they formed a ring with their wings around it like the Saturn rings."

Santiago could just picture that as he sat there looking up at the ceiling, completely clueless as to what his brother could see above him.

"White fluffy clouds also surrounded the sun and covered it in some parts, but because of the heat, it turned the clouds dark and menacing. The clouds began to spin along with the birds, enveloping the sun completely. The sun got completely covered by the clouds and wind. The only thing left was a hurricane of clouds, winds, and rain."

Sebastian kept looking up at the spinning clouds above him and let himself go. His eyes closed as the words coming out of his mouth slurred. The room went quiet. Santiago had already fallen asleep moments before.

The first week at the beach came and went pleasantly and quietly. Michelle and her husband seemed to be getting along a lot better there at the beach house. Michelle took her children to the beach every day at 10 a.m. for a few hours and returned back to the beach most days after 4 o'clock. On weekends, more people visited from the city and this first weekend after their arrival was no different.

Many beach houses were now filled with people, including the Swiss village chalet rentals down by the shore. That Saturday, it was a particularly cool day, and both Esteban and Michelle decided to take their kids to the beach in the early afternoon to take advantage of the ocean breezes.

On the way down the steps and as they passed the Swiss chalets, they noticed a man standing near one of the houses. The man was older than Esteban, perhaps in his sixties or seventies. He was washing the sand off of himself with a garden hose. There was a cooler with ice and a couple of leftover beer bottles scattered over the floor around him. Sebastian and Santiago noticed that the man was acting peculiar, like their father when he drank. As they neared the chalets, the man took off his swimming trunks and washed himself without care for who was watching. The children covered their mouths in shock, laughing and pointing at the naked man. He didn't care who saw him. As they saw this, their father, pushed his children and wife forward to avoid making eye contact with the man who just stood there as if he wasn't doing anything wrong. The man looked around and laughed incoherently as if something else had amused him. A few steps away from the scene, Sebastian looked up at his parents who both covered their faces with embarrassment for the man. Sebastian turned to look back at the man and noticed that he was grabbing his penis and pulling on it. As the man did this, an older blonde woman came around from behind a parked SUV next to the chalet and started screaming at the man, pulling his pants up as he turned the hose on her. Sebastian had never seen anything like that and ran ahead to meet back with his family. He grabbed both his parent's hands and pulled them forward to make them walk faster toward the beach.

That evening in bed, Sebastian and Santiago discussed the suspicious man at the Swiss chalet.

"Have you ever seen another man naked, San?"

His brother replied, "No, that's the first time, did you see how he pulled on his penis?"

Santiago answered with a question, "Did you see how purple it looked? Disgusting."

After a moment, Sebastian started again, "Today was fun, no? I like it when dad comes with us to the beach."

He received an affirmative nod from his brother.

"Remember the other day and the snake in the water? Imagine what would have happened if the snake bit one of us. I sure hope not, it would have been painful, no?" Santiago shuddered at the thought.

"I bet." Sebastian answered in the middle of a yawn, as he turned in the direction of his brother.

"That reminds me of that movie we saw a while ago, remember *20,000 Leagues Under the Sea*, and the giant octopus that attacked the submarine. When I go under the water in the ocean, I imagine that I am the submarine and that the animals are gigantic. I get to see all these different schools of small fish moving together in one direction away from me when they see me coming. They make these psychedelic patterns in the water to attract my attention. Then, two dolphins come to either side of my steel armature, they look at me and push their way forward ahead of me as if trying to secure a path in the water for my safety. From the darkness of the ocean, I suddenly see bright lights coming from all directions ahead of me, faint at first, but then becoming brighter by the second. The source is not noticeable at first."

Santiago was listening fully to his brother's story, and asked, "What is it Sebastian?"

Looking at the pictures of sea life framed on the wall above him, he picked out a scientific sketch, then replied, "They are sea horses! There appears to be lights coming out from their manes, all the way down to their tails, it is so beautiful."

He continued quickly, "The colors range from ultraviolet to light blues and change as they move in the water like waves up and down their bodies. I stop completely, suspended in the water on my own now since the dolphins have moved away past me. The waves of light emitting from the sea horses are captivating, almost hypnotic. My eyes start to feel like they are crossing as I watch all of this happening in front of me. The sea horses start to approach me slowly. I am not scared of them at all. Once they have circled me, I begin to see rays of blue light coming from above me. I am actually reaching the surface of the water by now. When I come to look back at the sea horses, they have already taken off toward the bottom of the ocean. I look up again and reach the surface. Instead of seeing the sky above, all I can see above the surface is a layer of clouds. There was something in the distance that appeared to be the peak of a mountain, all surrounded by clouds."

Santiago asked his brother, "Were you flying?"

Sebastian responded in the same quiet voice he had been using all along, "Yes, it was as if I was flying. I still had the protective steel armature that protected my body when I was underwater, but now it had been transformed into a flying container with wings and I was just simply flying above cotton-like clouds. Then, these bizarre looking animals appeared from within the clouds in different locations. It was dark so I couldn't see exactly what they were at first. There appeared to be a little bit of light in the distance toward the east. The animals moved in a strange fashion, like the jellyfish we see here at the beach sometimes. They are flying in the air above the clouds just like me. The space we are in seem darker above us and lighter toward that point in the east. If I turn to look above me, I can see a multitude of stars. I have finally reached a mountain peak to be able to get a clearer view and notice snow on the ground on some parts, otherwise the exposed earth is red. It is starting to get easier to see, as there is more light appearing in the sky. I can't see what is below the clouds but now I can get a better feel for the environment around me. The jellyfish all seem to be attracted by the source of light and traveling in its direction. I then see rays originating from that light source. A giant ball of fire peeks up from behind the clouds, it is huge and round, and the funny thing is that I can see it without it hurting my eyes."

By now, Santiago had been quiet for a while. Sebastian turned to look and saw that Santiago may had fallen asleep. He called on his brother without making too much noise.

"Yea." Santiago responded with his eyes closed. He was half asleep by now. Sebastian stopped talking and turned his head to look up at the ceiling. The swirl of clouds was there, ever present and looming over his body. He rubbed his eyes to clear his vision and when he opened them again, he saw thousands of colorful dots over the swirl of clouds. Everything went dark.

On Sunday, the children were excited to have their aunt Justine and Camilla over for a few days. They expected to go to the beach town chapel for service, but their father didn't feel like getting up early. Once they were up and ready to go to the beach, the kids had to wait for the visitors to arrive even though it was already way past their beach time. They were not very amused as they had gotten so used to the daily beach routine. The hammocks were rocked back and forth by the breezes that came through the house, as they waited.

Finally, a noisy car came turning from the street into the parking area in front of the house. Aunt Justine and Camilla had arrived. Camilla came out running toward Michelle and Esteban before the car came to a complete stop. She was happy and excited to see them all. Blanche, who was sitting outside by the hammocks reading a book, had her arms wide open to welcome Camilla, just as she did when welcoming her own grandkids. Camilla ran over to her and responded with an equally warm hug. Aunt Justine finally made it out of the car by then, and walked over to the house. Standing up for a while, she shared details about a traffic jam on the way to the beach. The adults sat by the dining room table outside while the boys took Camilla to see the pineapple field their parents prohibited them from playing near because of the pointy thick leaves. Then they took her to the field on the west side of the house where they could run around and play ball. After they were done, they ran back in the house and asked their parents if they could go to the beach. Since they were not able to go alone, they waited for Michelle, Justine, and Blanche to get ready. Their dad stayed behind watching a soccer game on the television and drinking his rum and cokes.

At the beach that day, the ladies sat on the sand over towels placed in a triangular shape. They sat facing the beach and watched as the children ran back and forth following the motion of the white foamed waves.

From the distance, the kids noticed a man walking toward them with a couple of horses. Santiago sprinted over to his mom and asked if they could ride the horses. Sebastian wasn't sure if his parents could afford the fee, which was twenty dollars per horse for thirty minutes, but he waited to see how his mom would react. Michelle thought it would be great distraction for the kids but asked the man if they could bring the horses by the house the next day so that the children could ride in the field next to the house. It took some convincing for Santiago to understand, but after Sebastian and Camilla agreed, Santiago gave in.

The next morning arrived, a perfect day for horseback riding, which was the only thing the kids could think of. The bees were out and about in the house garden, while the breeze gently rocked the hammocks. At nine, the two locals and three horses waited outside of the gate while Justine gathered the children. Michelle walked over to open the gate doors. The children had just finished breakfast and were as excited as if it were Christmas day. There were two brown horses and the third was white with dark brown spots all over. Camilla liked the spots on that horse and approached it first before Santiago or Sebastian could decide. After the boys chose their horses, Esteban and the other two men helped the children mount up. Once seated on their saddles, the men taught the children one by one how to make the horses go forward and how to turn left and right and most importantly, how to make the horses stop. Sebastian appeared to be apprehensive about the horse he was riding because it wasn't following orders, unlike the other two horses. The men took the horses from the driveway to the field next to the house while the other adults took photographs of the children.

The horses stood by the entrance to the field while their owners released them to walk on their own. Sebastian's horse wouldn't stay still and he didn't know what to do to make it stop. Santiago and Camilla's horses began to walk slowly forward around the field, while Sebastian's horse just kept moving backwards and around without following any of the orders that Sebastian was asking it to follow. He became uncomfortably scared. The older man in the straw hat noticed and darted over to pacify the horse. As the man approached, the horse took off running past the other two horses and around toward the pineapple field. Sebastian was so confused and frightened at this point, he didn't know what else to do but to scream at the horse to stop. He could also hear his parents telling him to stop the horse but to no avail. Michelle, Justine, and the others came running from their viewing spot into the field. Both Camilla and Santiago stood there looking at the crazy horse running around, both with their mouths wide open. Santiago, noticing that the horse was running toward the prickly pineapple plants, screamed at his brother to make the horse stop. Sebastian felt his little body jump up and down over the giant animal while it kept heading toward the pineapples. He panicked, looking over to his parents while pulling on the reins, but the horse would not stop.

He found a sudden supernatural amount of energy come into his arms as he tried one more time to pull on the reins. The animal finally stopped and pulled back at the very edge of the drop into the field. Sebastian could actually see the spikes from the pineapple leaves pointed toward him as if waiting to strike. By this point, the horse's owner and Michelle had arrived and both asked Sebastian if he was alright. He was shaking on the horse's back. The horse owner pulled the boy off the horse and handed him over to his mother in one quick motion. The man apologized and said that his horse had never acted like that before. He then told Michelle that he would not charge them for the rentals. Michelle took Sebastian back to the cabana while Blanche and Esteban gathered the other children and headed back to the house. The two men left with the horses quickly after the incident.

Sebastian said to his mother as he walked back to the house, "I thought the horse was going to jump into the pineapple field and hurt me."

"I saw you pulling on him, but nothing happened. That horse was crazy!" Responded his mother.

"Are you okay?" Asked his brother as they all approached the house. Santiago sat next to Sebastian on the hammock.

"Yes, I'm okay, just a little shaken. I thought the horse

was not going to stop; he was going so fast." Sebastian then laughed to lighten the mood.

He then said, "It was actually fun, but scary too."

Justine and Camilla went back home two days later, but this time, they took Blanche with them. It was incredibly quiet once everyone went home. The houses at the end of the street were all quiet as well. Sebastian and Santiago kept with their routine of combing the sand for treasures in the mornings, and sand castle building during the afternoon trips to the beach.

The sunny days and happy breezes from the ocean kept the beach at a pleasant temperature all year round but this time of year especially. Every night, their father would cook something on the grill by the cabana. It was either hamburgers, hot dogs, or Argentinian sausages. On a special occasion, he would grill fresh caught fish, mostly on weekends when family and friends came over to spend the day.

The next Tuesday, the whole family went to the beach in the afternoon. It was overcast and only a few glimpses of the sun could be seen at times. It was perfect for Michelle as she worried about her children getting too much sun, but by now they all showed signs of tans from the frequent visits. On the way back to the house, their dad told them he had a surprise for them. He was going to cook shrimp on the grill with some fish he had gotten from the local fish chap. Once at home he set up the grill while the children took a shower to get the sand off. The smell of the grill was hypnotic. Sebastian loved to eat seafood and could eat shrimp every day if he had the chance. Santiago also enjoyed a good shrimp cookout.

They both came out running into the cabana where their dad was standing grilling the food. Sebastian threw himself onto the hammock while grabbing either side of it, yet the hammock didn't open properly as he expected. He fell backwards, with the back of his head slamming into the edge of the cabana's concrete foundation. Michelle, who was inside of the house folding the clean laundry, heard a loud bang followed by a scream and unusual commotion coming from the cabana. She ran out to see her husband picking up Sebastian off the ground. He was crying and holding the back of his head. Once he moved it away, his fingers were filled with blood. A lot of it was coming out of the back of his head. Michelle screamed and immediately ran back in the house to look for something to put on the back of her son's head. Her husband carried Sebastian inside of the house while Santiago just followed along to see what was wrong with his brother. Michelle grabbed a white towel from the clean pile she had just folded and rolled it several times to form a shape that could be placed on the back of Sebastian's head to stop the opening from bleeding any further. Santiago heard his parents blaming each other for the accident while Sebastian just squealed loudly as if he was in the most horrible pain of his life. Michelle pulled the towel away from his head to expose the wound and noticed a gush of blood coming out of it without any sign of slowing down. She concluded that they needed to take Sebastian to the hospital, but where? The closest clinic was in a town about 30 minutes from the beach.

Before they had time to think, they were in the VW driving to the clinic in the next town. Santiago sat on the back of the bug, while his dad drove. Michelle held Sebastian in her arms while holding a much larger white towel on Sebastian's wounded head. Michelle kept telling Sebastian to stay awake and pushed on the towel so that her son wouldn't bleed to death. She felt the journey to the clinic to be the longest of her life. Everything slowed down in the car, Esteban looking over his injured son next to him, holding that life in his hands, while driving as fast as he could. Santiago in the backseat was just holding on for dear life and trying to keep calm while his parents rushed his brother to safety. Michelle held her son as hard as she could, a tear streaming down her cheek as she looked tenderly at her child's face. She prayed out loud that they would get to the clinic before something worse could happen. Sebastian sobbed. Facing the window. Through the tears in his eyes he could see shapes that resembled blurs of clouds and he kept hearing his mother tell him not to go to sleep.

After 15 minutes on the road, they arrived to the Rio Hato clinic. It was a small two room building painted in a beige color. A man with a black bag, a white guayabera shirt, and black pants was walking out of the building when the car approached the parking area. The man stopped when he saw Michelle and Esteban run out of the car with Sebastian, the towel was now completely drenched in blood and dripping off her arms. Esteban screamed at the man telling him they had an emergency and asked if the doctor was in.

"I am the doctor, I was just finishing my shift." The man responded. He quickly dropped the bag he was carrying and opened his arms as a signal to transfer their son to him so he could be taken inside. He carried the boy inside the clinic and rushed to put him on a bed face down in order to inspect the wound. A nurse walked in the room urgently with some medical instruments and laid them neatly on a rolling table next to the bed where Sebastian had been laid. As the doctor inspected the wound, he quickly realized that Sebastian needed stitches and explained to his mother that he would have to give her son a tetanus shot. His dad and Santiago stayed outside in the waiting room. Sebastian was crying out in pain the whole time, and when he heard the doctor say that he would need a shot, he became afraid and cried even louder. Esteban and Santiago could hear him all the way outside in the waiting room. Michelle held his hand while the doctor gave him the shot in the area of the wound. He yelled even louder than before. Michelle cried along with him as the doctor proceeded to clean the wound and prepare it for stitching. He said that they were lucky because he had just finished his day and was heading home when they arrived. She thanked him for staying and continued talking to her child to console him in his pain. She was devastated to see her son in this position. One stitch, two stitches, and so on. It took eight stitches to close the wound on the boy's head.

Once the doctor completed the surgical procedure, he left Sebastian to rest in the room while he walked Michelle outside to the waiting room. There, they met with Esteban and Santiago. The doctor explained what he had just done to close the wound, how to clean it and what medications to give him to help with infection and pain. Santiago just looked up at their parents and wondered if Sebastian was alright. As the doctor spoke to them, Santiago pulled on his mother's bloody shirt and asked how Sebastian was doing. She held his hand and knelt to his height, wrapped her arms around him and responded, "Yes, your brother is fine. He is just resting now. The nice doctor here gave him some stitches and told us he is going to be okay."

Santiago responded only with tears in his eyes while giving his mother a tight hug.

The night had come and everyone was safely back at the beach house. Michelle moved Sebastian and his brother to Blanche's bedroom so that they would be more comfortable. Sebastian laid down on his stomach as the doctor had instructed him to do. He was scared to move his head, thinking that if he did, the stitches would come off and he would bleed to death. He slept the rest of the afternoon. His mother walked in the room every 30 minutes to check on him. Sebastian's father was able to save some of the grilled food and finished cooking it for dinner that evening. He helped prepare the table with Santiago while Michelle walked quietly into Sebastian's room to wake him up to see if he wanted to eat something for supper. She sat next to him on the bed and caressed his cheek. He opened his eyes and asked his mother for water, then said that he wasn't hungry. She brought him some saltine crackers with butter and water so that he would have at least something in his stomach.

That evening, Sebastian heard his brother walk in the room and get in the other bed. He was quiet enough while Sebastian laid there with his eyes closed. Sebastian asked his brother what time it was, and Santiago responded that it was eight in the evening. Santiago covered himself and turned on the bed to face his brother.

He quickly asked, "How are you feeling, Seb?

Sebastian replied, "Tired, and it does hurt a little. I don't even want to move because it feels like my head weighs a thousand pounds."

Santiago didn't seem to understand but expected that his brother wouldn't feel like dancing around after the accident. Santiago stayed quiet a little while and then asked his brother if he was going to survive.

"I sure hope so. When our parents were taking me to the hospital, I kept seeing these clouds in the sky and a reflection on the window from the sun. It felt like I was dreaming, or was I not? The clouds kept making these odd shapes like flags moving in the wind. But the strangest thing of all is that even though it was daytime, the stars were all out and I could see them twinkling in the sky. From the distance, a far distance away, I could hear the faint sound of mom telling me not to go to sleep or close my eyes. But my eyes felt heavy and my body felt completely at ease."

Santiago responded, "I was scared and didn't know what to do."

Sebastian continued, "I was too, but it was almost like I didn't feel the pain anymore as the stars shined around me. For a moment, everything turned to white but then I felt a rush of movement and pain returned as I opened my eyes and saw a man that I had never seen before holding me and taking me into a building."

Santiago responded, "That was the doctor."

"Yes, I realize that now, but I didn't know who he was at first and didn't understand what he was doing. I do remember laying on a bed and crying because the pain was so unbearable."

Sebastian went on and on for a while explaining to his brother what it had been like to be in his place. Then there was quiet in the room. Sebastian couldn't see his brother from the direction he was laying on the bed so he assumed Santiago had fallen asleep. He tried to look up by moving his head a little to the left, but the movement brought back some of the pain. He tried again and was finally able to get a glimpse of the swirling clouds over him. He could see the faint outer edges of white soft clouds moving slowly being pulled inward from the energy within the ceiling of the room.

"What are you doing, Sebastian?" Asked Santiago, who was still awake looking over at his brother.

Sebastian jumped off the bed more surprised about his brother's sudden voice than the question itself.

"Do you see the clouds in the ceiling?" He responded.

Santiago looked up to the ceiling to see a pendant light that faintly illuminated the room moving slowly from side to side.

"What are you talking about? Don't be silly, Sebastian."

Sebastian didn't respond but tried to turn his head over to see his brother and couldn't do it. He felt his brother walk over to the other side of the bed and got his face close to Sebastian's. He looked at him with his big green eyes and asked, "Are you alright, Sebastian? Do you want me to call mom?"

A tear dripped down the side of Sebastian's cheek.

"No Santiago, I am okay, I just don't want to move my head because I am scared."

Santiago got on the bed with Sebastian and laid there

next to him until both fell asleep.

In the living room that evening, both Michelle and Esteban spoke about Sebastian's accident and decided to pack up and take the kids back home the next day, cutting their trip short by a week.

In the morning, they shared the news with the kids. Both were disappointed about the change in plans but they never expected something like this to ever happen to them anyway. Later that afternoon, Michelle packed the bags while her husband transferred them into the car. She made sandwiches for the kids and brought one over to Sebastian where he was still laying down on his stomach. He moved slowly to avoid any pain. His mother brought him a glass of water and antibiotics for him to take and then told him that she was going to clean the wound. He was not happy about that but the cleaning wasn't as dramatic as he made it seem. He watched *The Flintstones* cartoons during the day in the room while his brother played outside. At siesta time that afternoon, Santiago asked his brother to tell him more about the day before.

"When dad was driving to the hospital, I could see panic in mom's eyes. She was pretty scared while she kept pressing on my head. I was scared too. As I moved my eyes to look outside at the passing trees and clouds in the distance, my eyes got filled with the light from the sunshine and I was not in the car anymore. It felt as if I was standing in the middle of the sea."

Santiago asked, "Were you standing on the water?"

"Yes. I held the back of my head with my right hand and felt it was completely wet but it didn't feel like water. When I looked at my hand, it was filled with blood. I could see the blood rolling down the front of my body. It was tranquil over the water where I was inexplicably standing, not like at the beach with the surf, just weirdly still. In the distance, I could see the wind brush through the water and create small wave patterns that dispersed quickly. I was just standing there in the brightest of days with the sun in the distance. The clouds in the sky turned dark quickly and suddenly swirled right above me in a menacing shape. The vortex of clouds moved downward toward me, I could not see anything other than the clouds, the ocean below me, and the huge round shape of the sun. The wind picked up and pushed the sun down toward me. Everything turned bright as the whitest white you have ever seen."

Santiago interrupted his brother, "Did it burn?"

"No, I didn't feel anything, not even pain, the pain from my head had gone away. Then the oddest thing happened. The sun sat right above me inside of the vortex that now wrapped me alone in the middle of this quiet ocean. Next, the sun began to shrink to the size of a penny. Even though it was small, the brightness it emitted was just as if it was the original size. I looked up as I felt a rush of air like the blow dryer when mom dries her hair. The sun moved down in front of my eyes, and it blinded me. I couldn't see in front of me but could feel the heat radiating from it. The shape of the sun burned my retina and all I could see was the shape of the sun in a purple-green color surrounded by white everywhere. In all of this, I kept hearing voices telling me things, almost screaming. The miniature sun shape went around my head several times and after the third time, it went inside of me through the opening in the back of my head. I felt an immense painful feeling like an injection coming into my head at that moment. The light from the sun now inside of me surfaced all over my body and I could see the bones in my hands and arms as the light emitted outward from inside of me. Then everything turned black. When I opened my eyes again, I saw mom's face. I could see her moving her mouth but could not hear her. All I could hear was this high pitch sound in my ears from what I assume was the pain caused by the fall."

Sebastian stayed quiet for a while, then turned his head a little to see that his brother had fallen asleep as he frequently did by the end of his stories.

Softly almost to himself he said, "Santiago, the sun was inside of me." He then turned his head just a little to see the ceiling clouds, always circling, spinning over him as he fell asleep.

The End of Clouds

Children know. They may not know the reasons why, but they always know when something is wrong in the life of their parents. My brother and I knew. We felt the same pain and suffering that our mother felt. We didn't understand it, but we knew. Now that I am an adult, I ask myself, what gives a man permission to put down his wife because he has never learned to love? A man who does not even know how to love himself. He doesn't really even know what love is. How could a person like that ever love anyone else?

The warm breezes of summer turned slowly into humid rainy days, announcing a new school year. After the family returned home from the beach vacation, Esteban took his son to the doctor a couple of weeks later to check on the wound and everything seemed to be healing accordingly.

The doctor made a comment about removing the stitches, which concerned Sebastian. While in the car returning home that day, Sebastian asked his father what was going to happen to the stitches. His father, who really didn't know how to talk to his son, explained that they would return for the doctor to remove the stitches. His father then looked away to check out the woman in the car next to his. Sebastian just looked at his father and trembled from the idea of how the stitches would be removed. His head ached from the thought that he would have to go through that again. He could only imagine the experience would be as bad, if not worse, than the accident itself.

The uncomfortable evenings continued as Sebastian slept on his stomach to avoid hurting the wound. After a few weeks however, he ended up enjoying the new sleeping position with a different pillow his parents provided for him. The accident didn't stop him from sharing more wild stories with his brother, and while he couldn't really see the supernatural swirling clouds over his head, he could tell they were always there because he heard them and felt them close. He would open his eyes at times during the night and he would see lights flickering above him like miniature lightning bolts twinkling in the air. He would also see the reflections as the light would bounce off the white walls of the room as if to send him the message that they were still there looking over him.

One night a couple of weeks before the new school year started, past their bed time, both Santiago and Sebastian were still awake chatting. Neither were really sleepy that evening. Santiago brought up the new school year and that Sebastian would be starting secondary school.

"I don't know what to think about it." Said Sebastian.

"Mom says that it will be the same kids from the previous year that will be in the class but I won't believe it until I see it. I have to act differently."

Santiago asked, "Why? Like an adult?"

His brother responded, "No, I mean like I have to be taken more seriously. You see mom and dad; they act more like grandma. When did they have to start acting like that? I guess that's what I mean, you know they were children once and now they are adults. Does it change from one day to the next?"

Santiago didn't respond, just looked down at the floor

pondering on these deep thoughts his brother had.

"The classes I am going to take in secondary school seem hard. And like me, you'll also have to figure what to study for when you grow up."

Santiago still didn't say anything, then laid back on his back looking up and said, "I want to be a puppet master!"

Sebastian looked at him in disbelief. "Really Santiago?! I want to be a puppet master too. We could have a puppet theater and put on shows, like the shows we use to put together with Camilla at our grandparents house."

Sebastian explained all the details to his brother, the plays they would put on, how the theater looked inside, and how the puppets were dressed, but after a while he noticed that Santiago had fallen asleep.

A week before school started, Michelle took her children to the book store to get all the materials they needed for the new year, which included new uniforms to replace those they had outgrown.

At the store, each had a list of book titles they needed for their classes. For Santiago, the experience was fairly pleasant since he had seen the same books a couple of years before when his brother used them in school. There were also some new ones he had never seen. For Sebastian, it was a totally different experience. His books seemed to be thicker and heavier than ever before. He piled them up as his mother pulled them from the tables.

On the way to the car with the help of their mother, they all carried their individual purchases and set them on the back seat of the car. It was around lunch time, and Michelle decided to surprise her children by taking them over to see their dad at the office and then invite them all to lunch together. Michelle had never really done anything that adventurous. She thought to herself that it would be a nice surprise for her husband.

When they approached the hospital area, she drove down a path only reserved for hospital personnel and parked the bug in an empty spot a few steps away from the laundry facility where her husband worked. She removed the key from the ignition and asked her kids to accompany her. They all got out of the car and walked a few short steps to the entrance of the laundry facility. The space was open to the elements. There were large flat folding machines that women in uniforms used to fold enormous bed sheets on one end, while on the other end stood giant heavy duty washing machines. In the back to the right side, there was Esteban's little air-conditioned office. As Michelle walked in with the children behind her, she waved at some of the employees she recognized. Some of the women looked at her with invidious eyes, while others just turned to their colleagues and whispered. As she approached the office, she saw the door open wide and out came her husband holding hands with a woman she had never seen before. The woman was younger than Michelle and appeared to wear a hospital uniform with a name tag, but Michelle couldn't make out the name on it. As soon as she saw them appear, she turned around to stop her children and pulled them behind a column to avoid her husband seeing them. She whispered hurriedly to her children to run back to the car and that she would be there soon. Michelle looked around and noticed that a few of the workers looked away as they saw Esteban leaving his office with the unidentified woman. She then marched defiantly toward her husband.

Sebastian and Santiago ran back to the car and jumped in their seats as fast as they ever had before. Sebastian held his head after feeling dizzy from the sudden run, and checked on his healing wound by touching on it. Santiago, who was sitting in the back seat next to the school materials, inspected his brother's head and told him that his wound looked fine. They waited a few minutes when they saw their mom storming out of the facility with sun glasses covering her face and looking down as if ashamed, but visibly furious. She opened the door of the car and slammed it, turned the key in the ignition as fast as she could, hit reverse in her manual transmission and sped off.

She drove home, running stop signs and passing cars. Her children just sat in their seats holding onto anything they could and wondering what had happened. Michelle was quiet through the whole drive back home. Once at home, she ran into her room and slammed the door.

Sebastian and Santiago both trembled with confusion. They took their books and other materials and placed them on the dining room table, then ran into their bedroom, closing the door behind them. They sat on Santiago's bed and heard their mother's voice speaking loudly to someone on the phone. She screamed and cried as if something terrible had happened. They went without lunch or dinner that day. Their father never returned home that evening.

Later that night, after all had quieted down in the house, Sebastian and Santiago went over to the kitchen and made sandwiches with what they could find in the fridge. Sebastian had taken some of the school books into their room and browsed through them as they ate.

Between bites, Santiago asked his brother, "I am not entirely sure what happened today. Did you see how those ladies in dad's office looked at us?"

Sebastian replied, "Yes, I saw their faces, but I don't

know what happened. Did Mom see something bad? Where is Dad?"

Santiago just raised his shoulders in his peculiar way.

That evening, the house was very quiet, unusually silent for a house with young kids. Sebastian and Santiago got themselves into bed and as they did, they both felt an unspoken but vivid feeling of loneliness in the air. Sebastian, face down on his bed, looked over at his brother and noticed his blonde curls shine in the light that reflected from the outside into the room.

"Your eyes seem darker than I have even seen before."

Sebastian remarked, then continued, "Earlier today I happened to look at your eyes when we were at the book store and noticed them turn a dark olive green. It reminded me of a picture of the eclipse I saw in one of grandma's *National Geographic* magazines."

Santiago thought for a moment, "What is an eclipse?"

His sibling answered, "San, I thought you had seen the photos, I showed them to you."

Santiago replied, "I would remember what that was."

Sebastian continued, "I'll explain. There were these two kids, their names were San and Seb."

Santiago interrupted, "That's us. Is it us?"

Sebastian held his hand up in a motion to tell his

brother to let him continue, "No, they are two totally different kids. Anyway, the kids lived in an Alaskan mountain range."

Santiago interrupted again, "That is definitely not us. I wish we lived in Alaska where it is cold."

Sebastian continued, "So, they wore ten pound coats made of leather and other natural furs. Their feet were protected with these huge leather boots too, and wrapped with a special type of fur that looked different than the rest of their outfits. Their heads were also covered in furs, only a little of their faces could be seen from all these coverings. They walked as if they were used to the weight of those clothes on them. They were coming home from fishing all day, each one carrying two large salmon on their backs. As they walked up a hill toward home, the salmon bounced up and down on their backs in a silly manner as if they were still alive."

Santiago giggled imagining the leaping fish.

"The boys' red cheeks glowed over their faces. The sun glimmered as bright as their cheeks in the distance above a field of blue spruces lining the top of the hill. The snow-covered mountain where they lived reflected the sunshine into every direction creating shadows from the trees along the path where the boys were. The place smelled like an eternal Christmas. Although they were alone, they were self-sufficient."

Santiago interjected, "What is self fu-ssi-cient?"

Sebastian laughed and said, "No, it's self-su-ffi-ci-ent, it's like a person that doesn't need parents to take care of them, they can take care of themselves."

His brother asked, "So, where were they going?"

"They were heading home. Weren't you paying attention? Anyway, they suddenly stopped in their tracks when they heard a noise coming from the trees above."

His brother asked, bewitched by this new piece of information, "What was it?"

Sebastian continued, "They saw a large eagle, with a beautiful golden beak and long wings that seemed to spread for miles. The Inuit . . ."

Santiago interrupted once again, "Inu what?"

Sebastian replied, "Inuit, is a group of inhabitants of the Alaska peninsula."

Laughing, Santiago responded, "You are like a walking encyclopedia today."

Sebastian threw his pillow at Santiago, "Quit it."

Santiago threw the pillow back at Sebastian with even more force. Sebastian almost fell on the other side of the bed from the impact. He looked at Santiago, who could tell that Sebastian was getting upset.

"So, the Inuit boys thought it was odd that the eagle went the opposite direction from the kids, down the mountain instead of up as before. The older boy turned to look forward at the trail they still had left to walk to get home and pressed on his brother to continue on. To their surprise, they both saw the eagle returning and flying real close to them, as if trying to get their attention. Both boys thought that perhaps the eagle was looking to steal one of the salmon, yet it didn't appear to show an attacking posture. The boys continued on their journey. The older boy kept a visual track of where the bird was headed. The eagle flew in a circular path and from behind, returned to the area where the boys were, this time it flew so close that they could feel the cold air created by the wings. Both boys covered themselves and the little one even fell to the snow-covered ground to avoid colliding with the bird. The breeze was amplified by a strong gust of air that seemed to be coming from the base of the mountain. As the boys looked up to follow the bird flying above them and toward the mountain peak, they saw that past it, the sun was suspended there with a bite taken out of it. They couldn't imagine why this was happening. Perhaps they thought that it was similar to the moon when it appeared and disappeared in a span of days, but this was definitely different. The eagle vanished from site, and the wind calmed. The boys kept walking up toward their home keeping a close watch of what was happening to the sun above them. As they neared their humble cabin, they noticed how the sun was slowly disappearing from the sky as if something was erasing it."

Santiago asked in complete amazement, "How?"

Sebastian held his hand up again.

"So, the boys dropped their fishing equipment, the salmon and a carryall, and ran into their home where a woman appeared followed by the children. They all ran toward a patch where they could have full visibility of the sun. They all stopped in shock as, in front of their eyes, the sun only appeared to be a sliver, an eyelash thick. They could still see the roundness of it but the rest of its shape was completely eaten away. The shadows caused by the sun's location over the mountain disappeared completely in a matter of seconds. San, the younger boy looked up at his mother with a look of confusion as to what was happening while she extended her arm to reach over to him. She held him and let him stand in front of her, as Seb stood a few steps in front of them completely flabbergasted by what was occurring in front of his eyes. The shaving of sun left in the sky unexpectedly became a ring of light that radiated outward. They saw waves of light emitting outside of this hole that had eaten the sun in the atmosphere above them. The ripples of light came and went in strength, mimicking the rhythm of a heartbeat. It was a precious sight to see. Seb was so taken by this phenomenon, that he fell on his knees looking up and smiling, almost laughing in astonishment, pointing at the missing sun and looking back at his mother and brother. San was so impressed that his jaw just dropped and froze. The dark mountain created an eerie feeling of solitude over the three of them. The blaze of fire continued on for several minutes, thrusting waves of light and fire outward into the heavens. Then the ring evaporated just like it appeared, and the sun started to re-appear very slowly. It felt like a second sunrise, even though the sun was already high up in the firmament. Darkness slowly became light again, the Inuit began to see the trees create their normal shadows on the snow once again. The sun above appeared like a splinter at first, but on the opposite side than where it had been before. The children felt at ease seeing the sun re-emerge like magic above them. San, whose vision had been fixed on the apparition, turned to his mother wondering what had just happened."

Santiago stood up on his bed and shrieked with delight,

with no regard for others who were sleeping. "So that's what it looks like when we cover the sun?"

His brother responded, "Yes, Santiago!"

Sebastian got up on his bed and together both jumped on their mattresses causing the pillows to tumble on the floor. Then both jumped onto each other's mattress at the same time, then again until they did it several times. They both fell on the beds giggling quietly to avoid a visit from their mother, or even worse, from their father if he was back at home. But they both knew that this was highly improbable. Both Santiago and Sebastian got out of their beds and pressed their ears onto their bedroom door trying to listen in for any sound coming from the hallway. They looked at each other as if trying to communicate telepathically. Nothing could be heard on the other side of the door. They went back to their beds and settled for the night. It was 10:30 by then. Santiago fell asleep pretty quickly, while Sebastian rattled on for some time more about the Inuit children and how he wished he could see snow someday. He covered himself up to his nose and looked up to the spinning cloud above of his room.

By now his stitches had healed well enough to be able to sleep comfortably on his back again, but he still felt some odd uncomfortable feeling on the back of his head at times, as if he still had the stitches. It was a creepy feeling that made him shiver at times. The cloudy swirl over him appeared to be more active than other nights. Sebastian even had a peek at what appeared to be beyond the clouds. He had never been able to see so clearly past the thick layers of gray, white, and black clouds. For a very short time, he saw a patch of sky, as if the ceiling wasn't even there. Before the clouds moved on to cover the patch, he saw a star further up.

The school year became a blur, and before they knew it, the children were already through the third term. At least it felt like a blur for the children who had so much to learn and so many events to participate in. The best time of the year before Christmas was quickly approaching. October welcomed Sebastian and Santiago's birthdays. Having been born a day apart, within 2 years from each other, their parents always celebrated both birthdays with a huge party. This year, Michelle surprised her kids with a Halloween-theme party celebration. And while they jumped up and down as children usually do, they became completely ecstatic when their dad shared that the party would be held at Urraca Park.

The kids counted the days to their birthday celebration.

Every night before bedtime, they would ask their mother how many days it was until their birthday party. While the boys worried about what costumes to wear for the party, their parents sent out invitations, arranged and put together parting gifts for the guests, and ordered the birthday cake and food to feed fifty adults and children.

The birthday party took place on Saturday, October 17. That Saturday morning, Michelle and Esteban went into their children's room quietly in order to avoid waking them up, however Sebastian was already awake by the time they stepped in the room. He had not slept all night with the anticipation about the day to come. When he noticed his parents in the room, they both rushed to Sebastian's bed and softly sang happy birthday to both kids. By the end of the song, Santiago was awake and sitting with his parents on Sebastian's bed. Sebastian removed the gift wrapping carefully from the large box of magic tricks.

"Wow, that's just what I wanted!" He exclaimed as if he had just won the lottery.

His father helped him open the box to expose ten different tricks lined beautifully inside. He quickly removed the magic book from the box and started flipping through it. They all sat on his bed for a few more minutes while viewing the large box of tricks. Then it was Santiago's turn to open his gift. Michelle held a large oddly shaped wrapped gift that was too large to fit on the bed. It sat next to the bed on the floor. She handed Santiago his gift and gave him a warm hug and kiss on his cheek.

"I hope you like your birthday gift."

He ripped the paper off the box in the same manner his brother had done moments earlier.

"Awesome, I got the guitar I wanted! Dad, are you going to teach me how to play?"

"Yes, son." He replied.

Santiago saw the shiny guitar behind the box cover with a transparent opening, an amazing sight. He rushed to open the box and held his new guitar like a mother holds her baby for the first time.

"Thank you!" He screamed as he hugged the guitar and played for a few moments enjoying his new toy.

"We need to get ready for the party. I need to go pick up your grandma and then pick up the cake and the food for the party." Michelle then continued while looking at Esteban, "You are getting the ice and taking the drinks for the party, right?"

He nodded in agreement.

When the children arrived to the party, they were already wearing their costumes. Santiago in a cowboy outfit complete with hat and boots. His father even bought him a belt buckle with longhorns on the front, and a toy cowboy set complete with holster, and plastic revolver. Santiago said that it reminded him of his Big Jim action figures. Sebastian, who was fond of Halloween, wore a Dracula outfit enhanced with red cape and fangs. His face was painted black and he accentuated his eyes by adding red around the sockets with red lipstick.

The boys rushed out of the car and ran to check out the rides. A section was decorated for Halloween; everything was orange and black. Balloons of the same colors framed the space where the celebration was to take place. There was a table with the biggest cake they had ever seen depicting Dracula's castle on one side and a scene from the wild west with a cowboy on a horse on the other side. It was the funniest thing they had ever seen but that's what they wanted after all. On the left side of the tables by the horse carousel, in an open field with a wooden floor were the two piñatas hanging side by side; a giant orange pumpkin with classic triangular eyes and a big smile, and across from it, a giant knife in gray and black. The knife piñata even had a glossy finish on the cutting edge that reflected the bright sun that shined that morning onto the park. Both piñatas looked like they were ready to burst with candy and toy surprises inside. To their delight, there were a couple of their school mates at the park by the time they arrived. Benjamin, their neighbor across the street from the apartment, arrived next and not far behind came aunt Justine and their cousin Camilla wearing a yellow and white clown outfit. She appeared to be upset.

Esteban joked, "Are you an angry clown?"

She didn't respond.

Justine then reached over to the kids and gave them both their gifts, which appeared to be the same odd shape and wrapped exactly the same. They both thanked her and as they questioned where to put the gifts, Michelle hollered from the cake table where she appeared to be organizing the plates and silverware for the food.

"Place the gifts over on this table by the cake."

There was a square table she had brought from home with a couple of gifts on it already. The table was even covered with a Halloween-theme disposable tablecloth.

Once Camilla saw her cousins, she smiled and ran over to them.

"I like your costume, Camilla!" Said Sebastian while his brother approved with a nod.

"When can we ride the carousel?" Camilla asked.

They all looked up at their parents in harmony.

"Let's wait a little while for more guests to arrive." Michelle responded.

She then walked over with Justine to where several of the adults were already mingling. Blanche and Esteban were both chatting when Justine and Michelle approached. Once about twenty kids had arrived to the party, the children began to enjoy the rides. There was a train that went around and around, as did the popular carousel with wooden horses that had seen better days.

At 12:30 sharp, Michelle called on all the children to stand by the cake to sing to the birthday boys. Their father took pictures. Sebastian, Santiago, and Camilla all stood next to each other with their friends dressed as Goblins, Superman, Scarecrow, and even a Mickey Mouse, standing behind the birthday table posing for photos. The gift table was overflowing, and so was the amount of kids standing there behind the cake. After the photos, Michelle lit all the candles she could get on the large cake and called on the kids to sing the happy birthday song. Blanche helped in cutting the cake and passing the slices out to the children.

The piñatas followed. It was a frenzy of energy; the children wishing to hit and break the piñatas down one at a time. First was the Pumpkin. Children stood in line behind Sebastian who went first, followed by Santiago and so on. With a large wooden stick, they took their turn hitting the piñata three times. After five kids had their turn to whack the piñata, it was ready to burst. Esteban grabbed the pumpkin from its top opening and split it in half like it was tissue paper. Candy, gum, chocolates, small cars, and toy soldiers tumbled onto the floor and in every direction. The children went wild trying to grab as much candy and gifts as possible. Even some of the adults got on the floor to grab candy for the smaller kids. Then in the same manner, the knife piñata was hit by the children which broke much easier. More candy and small toys sprung out of the piñata and onto the hair of children who were already on the floor in anticipation of the bounty they were to discover.

At around three o'clock the party started to wind down. Friends of Michelle and Esteban stayed behind with their children. Aunt Justine and Camilla had already left by then. Blanche and some of the men helped Michelle move the gifts from the table onto the small VW luggage compartment and on the back seat, quickly realizing that they would not fit along with the children. Hank, one of Esteban's closest friends offered to take the rest of the gifts in his car, and so the party ended on that note.

Once at home, Esteban continued to drink and appeared fully intoxicated. However, this time, instead of being loud and obnoxious, he was dismissive and detached from everyone. He just sat there while the children opened their gifts one by one.

Michelle would pass on each of the wrapped gifts and read the card out loud. She kept the cards to one side of the dining room table in an organized pile, while Blanche kept a list of names of everyone who had brought a gift.

"Another Topo Gigio doll!" Exclaimed Sebastian to Santiago as he opened one of his gifts.

"This one opens and closes his eyes, look!" Responded Santiago to his brother.

Santiago placed it on the floor right next to him.

"That was a gift from your grandmother," Said Michelle to her son while she smiled.

"Do you like it Santiago?" Inquired Blanche.

Santiago quickly responded, "Yes, Grandma, it is cool!"

"What do you say, Santiago?" Asked his mother.

"Thank you, Granny." He stood up and walked over to her to give her a hug.

They wanted to play with everything at the same time, but Michelle reminded them to finish opening the rest of the gifts before deciding what to play with first. The gift opening party continued on for about a half hour. By then, Benjamin, their neighbor and Hank had all left.

Esteban disappeared into his bedroom, while the boys changed into their regular clothes. They ate leftover party food and cake and recollected the highlights of the birthday party with their mother and grandmother.

The Dark Side of the Sun

Is there a dark side of the sun? We always wondered if there was and if the dark side was hell where the devil lived. It had to be. To us, bad things happened on the dark side of the Sun.

The school year rushed and the children looked forward to Christmas, still about a month and a half away.

Michelle and Esteban continued to expose their children to loud fights about Esteban's drinking problem which had grown into a consistent schedule of visits to the bar. The children didn't quite understand all of this, and focused their attention on school and their friends.

New neighbors from across the hall moved in and they quickly became friends. They also met other kids from down the street at another apartment complex a block away. They would all get together and play in the rain splashing each other with the falling water, a welcome gift in the Panamanian ever-present heat. They played hide and seek, and misbehaved as children habitually do by hiding behind stairwells and scaring adults coming from work. They would run so fast and hide where they could so that the adults wouldn't know who they were or where they went. Santiago got into the most of all trouble, both in school and in the neighborhood.

One Saturday that Fall, Santiago, Sebastian, Benjamin, and another one of their friends named Rocky, found an out of order elevator with the door left wide open in the lobby of a neighboring apartment building. They bet each other to go in the elevator, close the door and stay in it for as long as possible. Santiago, who was scared of nothing, went in first without even thinking about it. Sebastian asked him not to but he still went in. Sebastian watched as the door closed with Santiago inside. Santiago couldn't see a thing but could hear his brother asking if he was alright.

"Yes, it's just dark and hot in here."

After waiting a few minutes, they asked him to come out but the door would not open.

"I can't seem to get out. Press the button from the outside." Suggested Santiago.

Sebastian pressed the button outside of the elevator, but nothing happened.

"It doesn't open, Santiago." Sebastian pressed the button three times again with the same result. Santiago started to bang the door out of desperation and now was yelling for the attention of his brother and friends.

Benjamin, who was by now trying to pry the door open with his bare hands, asked if he could try pushing the buttons from the inside.

Santiago couldn't see a thing in front of him, but he thought that Benjamin's suggestion might work. He sensed the wall by the door where he was standing. With his fingers, he felt his way up to a section that had knobs and some indentations toward the right next to the door.

By now, he could actually see a little from the slit between the two doors, but it was very faint.

Sebastian, in the lobby continued to press the button while both Rocky and Benjamin tried pulling the door open with all his strength. Sebastian became incredibly nervous by now and just imagined how much trouble they would be in if their parents found out Santiago was stuck in the elevator.

Inside the elevator, Santiago continued to feel his way around the buttons and bumps that could potentially help him evacuate this unpredictable confinement. He pressed a button, but nothing happened. Through the sweat on his face, he could see a red button at the bottom, he pressed it and an alarm sound erupted and reverberated loudly inside the confines of the small space. He let go of the button and the alarm ceased.

Everyone outside screamed out loud. Then everything turned quiet for a moment. Sebastian and the others couldn't hear any noise coming from inside.

"Are you okay, Santiago? Santiago?"

He then waited for a moment but heard nothing.

Benjamin pulled on the door as hard as he could with Rocky's assistance. After trying without success, they stopped and were able to hear Santiago messing with the door from within.

Santiago continued pushing on every button he could feel, then he pulled a knob toward him, which made the door give in slowly bringing light and air into the elevator.

Benjamin and Rocky pulled the door open just enough to allow Santiago to shoot out like a bullet from a pistol.

Sebastian caught his brother as he escaped the elevator and both fell on the floor. They got up again and the four kids ran out of the elevator lobby as fast as they could. Sebastian and Santiago followed Rocky who lived in the same building, while Benjamin returned to his apartment across the street.

At home, their parents were nowhere to be found. Santiago gasped for air and sat on one of the balcony chairs asking his brother for some water. Sebastian ran to the kitchen, filled a glass full of water from the pitcher in the refrigerator and brought it back to his brother. They both sat on the same chair looking out of the balcony onto the street trying to catch their breath. Sebastian took Santiago's cup and drank what was left of the water. Out of the corner of the balcony door Michelle's head popped in, having heard her children run into the house.

"What's going on? Is everything okay?"

Sebastian turned to her and tried to sound reassuring.

"Yes, we were just downstairs, playing with Benjamin and Rocky."

Michelle's head popped back out without a response.

Later that night, as they both lied in bed, Sebastian asked his brother about the elevator.

"What was it like being inside it?"

"It was just dark and warm, Sebastian, and it smelled like sweat," responded his brother.

"Did something happen in there? We stopped hearing you for a moment and thought that maybe you passed out or something."

Santiago didn't know what he was talking about.

"We could hear you messing with the buttons, and I called you but you didn't answer back. Did you pass out?"

"No, Sebastian, nothing happened. I got a really bad headache from the heat but the next thing I knew I was just pulling on this knob on the wall that made the door open back again." Santiago answered.

"That is so weird. I am glad we didn't have to call Mom and Dad." Sebastian commented.

Santiago noticed Sebastian getting emotional about the elevator experience and asked him if he was all right.

"Yes, Santiago, I love you." Santiago got up from his bed and sat on Sebastian's bed and gave him a hug.

Once the lights went out in the room, the vortex of clouds and light show returned to the ceiling. Sebastian gazed at it for a while without saying a word, almost mesmerized by its power and magic. He would even count to see how long he would go without blinking, so that he could capture as much of the dizzying nightly display as possible. Unexpectedly, he saw a light source out of the corner of his right eye. It looked like a search light over the side of Santiago's bed. The light seemed to break apart from the thickness of the clouds above, yet still trying to come through it. The light was bright and heavy, similar to the laser light he had seen in a school exhibition a while back. He raised his right hand and pointed at the light.

"Do you see that, Santiago?"

But Santiago was already fast asleep.

"Santiago, Santiago! Do you see that light over you?"

No response came from him.

"I was going to tell you where the sun went next, but I guess we'll have to leave it for another night."

And the rains came as they always do when November approaches. The end of the year was looming and the humidity became ever more present. During this time of the year, Sebastian and Santiago along with his buddies, played on the ground floor of their apartment building under cover near the front entrance shielded from the rain. It was not a day to be playing in the rain as their parents had told them time and time before. Santiago wore his cowboy hat and belt to stay in character with the adventure they created in their heads.

They would get really close to the ground with their Big Jim and Big Joe, and played as if they were exploring a site on another planet away from Earth.

The planet was full of conical craters; a desolate lifeless land, they imagined. While taking their dolls over a patch of this brown dirt full of craters, they noticed a crater kept pushing dirt off the bottom of its narrowed end.

Santiago called out to his brother and friends and asked them if they had seen this happen before.

"Look at what happens when I drop a little bit of dirt into the bottom of this crater." They all knelt in a circle around the hole and waited to see what would happen. Then, out of nowhere they noticed the pellets of dirt get pushed out of the hole as if there was something underneath the ground pushing the dirt away. They all looked at each other, exclaiming at the same time, "Wow! That was awesome!"

"What was that?" Asked Sebastian.

They quickly assumed there was some type of animal

under the ground. The crater bug as they ended up calling it, was oddly shaped, as Santiago soon found out. He got a discarded paper cup and scooped a whole crater along with all the dirt around it. He then slowly spilled the dirt onto his other hand to see what would show up. He almost jumped when he saw a funny looking bug with a soft body, like nothing he had ever seen before. He laughed out loud as the animal tickled his hand. Sebastian and the other kids set aside their toys and followed Santiago's lead to find more crater bugs.

Sebastian was terrified of the bug and refused to hold it on his hand until his brother told him it tickled a little.

"Are these Mexican jumping beans?" Benjamin asked.

It was something they had seen and felt before.

By now each one had a crater bug in the palm of their dirty hands.

"I don't think so. How would they put the bugs inside of the shells?" Sebastian responded.

"I dunno. I think they are called ant lions or something like that; they eat other bugs." Said one of them.

Toward the end of that afternoon, once the rain had subsided, they saw the VW come into the driveway to the parking area in the back of the building. Both Sebastian and Santiago ran back to welcome their mother who had just returned from the supermarket.

"Hi Mom." They both saluted their mother.

"Help me with these grocery bags." Michelle noticed their hands and knees were soiled from playing in the dirt all day. Santiago's face in particular was a sight to see.

His mother pointed at him and asked, "What have you been getting into now, Santiago?"

"We were just playing in the dirt."

Each one helped her carry a bag all the way up to their apartment. Once upstairs, Santiago asked his mother to close her eyes and open her hand.

"What are you going to do to me, Santiago? You need to go wash."

"Just open your hand, nothing's going to happen." He reassured her while he placed an ant lion on the palm of her open hand.

She screamed. "Ay, it tickles, it tickles!"

Her arm jumped and the ant lion went flying and landed on the kitchen floor by the cabinets. Santiago ran over to the corner and picked it up with a napkin.

"Get that out of here, Santiago! Now!" All through this, Sebastian just stood there cracking up.

A couple of weeks later, Saturday, November 13 to be

precise, Esteban had already taken off to his usual bar round by eleven thirty that morning.

It was a hot and steamy day, unusually sunny for the time of year. There was only one cloud in the sky and a gentle breeze flowed through the quiet city. The tree limbs danced softly from one side to the other, while some of the leaves holding on for dear life gave up their fight and departed their place on the branch toward wherever the wind blew. Birds chirped happily on those trees across the street from the apartment building where Santiago and Sebastian lived. Only a few cars moved about the roads. In the morning, Santiago practiced his guitar lessons, repeating the same chord over and over, and getting better as time went by.

In the afternoon, Sebastian stayed in to watch *Sábados con Martinez Blanco* on the television. As he often did, he sat on the floor in front of their parent's bed and watched the show, taking comfort in the shaggy carpet below him and the cool air conditioner. His mom walked in the room after the program had already started, perhaps a half hour later, and laid down on her side of the bed.

Today, the program had a preview of a Toy land show the children enjoyed. A ballerina dressed in a white pollera showed selections from an upcoming musical about a cockroach queen which made no sense to Sebastian. After many loud commercial interruptions, Michelle got up and went to the kitchen to get a drink of ice water.

In the kitchen, she felt the heat of the day hit her like a wall. She grabbed a paper napkin from the napkin holder sitting next to the toaster and dried her face. She stood there for some time as she felt an unusual feeling come to her out of nowhere. She then went back to her well-ventilated room surprising Sebastian with a mango she had cut into several pieces. He was glued to the television when a Topo Gigio commercial appeared, a preview for an upcoming show they had not seen yet.

Abruptly, the door of the bedroom crashed open so hard that Michelle jumped off the bed. There, framed by the door, stood two children they both recognized, the children's playmates from down the street. The taller kid, holding a pair of shoes and extending them to Michelle, said almost losing his breath, "There's been an accident! Santiago has been in an accident!"

Sebastian stood up looking at the shoes and instantly connected in his mind that it was Santiago who had been in an accident. Michelle, who was already standing in front between Sebastian and the two other children, held her hand to her chest.

"What happened?! What happened?!" She screamed, "Where is Santiago? Sebastian, have you seen him?"

"Santiago, was in an accident." The boy responded.

She grabbed the shoes, one spilling on the floor and ran toward the door. Sebastian picked up the shoe as he followed the boys and his mother toward the front door.

"Come on Seb, let's go get your brother." She didn't know where to go or what to do, holding the one shoe near her chest she asked the boy, "Where is Santiago? What happened to him?"

The tall boy stopped and replied, "A car hit him, an ambulance took him to the hospital."

She was breathing so hard, she couldn't even talk anymore. "What ... Where ... did they ... take him?"

"I think to the Caja del Seguro Social!" Responded one of the boys.

She moved near to the boy and asked him, "Is he okay? Is he okay?"

"I don't know. I didn't see him being taken away."

She thanked the boys for letting her know and ran down the stairs without locking the door of the apartment. The children followed behind her.

In a flash, Michelle and Sebastian were inside of the Bug racing through the streets toward the hospital where her husband worked. She shook all over, her hands trembling the most. At a stop light, she looked over at Sebastian to see how he was doing. He was in shock, not understanding fully what had just happened. Michelle's eye liner watered and lined her cheeks all the way to her chin, but she didn't care how she looked, she just wanted to reach the hospital as soon as she could. The drive felt like a journey around the earth, although only lasted a couple of minutes, fifteen at the most. Sebastian didn't say a word throughout the whole trip to the hospital.

Once they arrived, she parked sideways between two parking spaces. She slammed the door behind her and reached out to her son to follow her into the emergency room. To Michelle's surprise, her husband was already there to meet them.

"Do you know what happened?" Asked Michelle.

"Santiago was hit by a car, that is all I know so far. He went to play over by the neighbor's house a block away from the apartment and he was playing on the side walk and apparently a woman came and hit him. The neighbor's mother called the apartment but no one answered so she tracked me down thinking you were already on your way."

Sebastian stood there next to his parents listening to all this and looking around the room to see if he could find his brother.

The room was white as white can be, with a gray-blue horizontal line that went all around the space. There was an old man with an IV sitting there and appeared to be more dead than alive. On the other side of the room was a woman, older than his mom, who was resting on a bed and didn't move at all. A lady and a man stood next to her holding the lady's hand. There were a couple of other people there, just sitting in the waiting area on square metal chairs with light blue vinyl cushions.

Michelle sat down completely drained from the rush of adrenaline that had propelled her to the hospital. "Did he break his hand, his foot? What happened?"

Michelle noticed her mother get out of a taxi cab by the emergency room entrance and got up to receive her.

"How did she find out?" Asked Michelle.

"I called her to let her know." Responded her husband.

Sebastian, who was sitting next to his mother, got up to go hug his grandmother and returned to his chair waiting for them to sit back down. Blanche sat next to her daughter while Esteban gave her the news.

"It looks like the woman tried to escape the scene when Santiago hit the windshield and then ..."

His eyes started to water. ". . . the lady stopped which

caused him to fall in front of the car. That's when she took off, carrying him under the car for seven houses. He's in surgery right now."

Blanche and Michelle sat there sobbing as they heard the details of the accident and thinking of the worst.

Blanche took Sebastian to the side and said, "Let's go get something to drink."

She looked at her daughter gesturing that she was going to take Sebastian away to protect him from hearing further gruesome details. Esteban was obviously less concerned about Sebastian hearing the awful news.

Sebastian and Blanche went up to the third-floor break room while Michelle and Esteban waited for news. Several hours later, Blanche spoke to Michelle and decided to take Sebastian to the apartment. She called a cab outside the emergency room and went home.

Meanwhile, at the hospital, Michelle and Esteban got a visit from one of Esteban's colleagues, Dr. Adames. He was a tall slim man with grayish hair and rectangular shaped glasses. He was not working that Saturday but went to the hospital to check on Santiago's status so that he could provide more information to his parents. The doctor came from behind the Post-Surgery Recovery doors looking down all the way to the waiting area.

"Santiago just got out of surgery and is in intensive care at the moment. He is in critical condition. His cranium is fractured in several places, he broke his arm in many places, as well as both his legs."

He then paused for a second thinking of how to share the next piece of information. "He is in a comma and cannot breathe on his own. Dr. Singh, a very good surgeon, has taken care of his head, arm, and legs, but your child needs more surgery. He'll be in intensive care for about forty-eight hours and then Dr. Singh will decide the best approach at that point."

Michelle just cried with folded arms as if she was freezing. Her husband wrapped his arm over her. She broke down and almost lost all her strength to the point that she had to be carried by the two men over to a chair in the corner of the waiting room where there was more privacy. She stayed there for a moment while the two men walked away toward the center of the room. She couldn't hear them but just imagined the worst.

Esteban, having worked in the hospital for so many years, had heard horrible stories of accidents and was more immune to the reality of this very moment, but it was a very different feeling when it came to his own son.

Dr. Adames spoke softly and looked away so that

Michelle wouldn't hear him as he gave a more realistic assessment to Esteban.

"It doesn't look good, my friend. I got to see him. Without the oxygen pump he would be dead already."

They stood there talking for a little bit more.

The hours just wouldn't move fast enough as Michelle sat there looking past everything in her line of vision. Esteban would bring her food but she wouldn't eat. He would bring her water or juice but she wouldn't drink. The hours turned to night and no news had been offered about their son. Esteban asked Michelle if she wanted to stay, and she just nodded yes while saying, "I am not leaving this place without my son."

She was quiet and thoughtful all throughout the evening because she had realized so many things about her life by her present situation. She wanted to be in control but this was completely out of hers.

That evening, Dr. Singh came out from the intensive care unit and brought Michelle and Esteban a much-needed update.

"Hello Esteban, Michelle. Your son just came out of the last surgery and is in post-operative care. He is going to be there for the next 48 to 72 hours and then moved to a room upstairs. He was hit pretty hard, but he was a trooper in surgery."

Michelle, who was still holding Santiago's shoes in her arms, began to sob again uncontrollably. She eventually quieted down enough to take some deep breaths and ask if he would be okay. "It is too early to tell. Let's pray for him. He's a strong little boy."

The phone rang late that night at around 10:45. Blanche answered it. Michelle was at the other end of the line. Blanche quietly just listened for a moment. She took the phone with her and sat down on the sofa.

"Okay dear, please be strong . . . Yes, Sebastian is fine, he is sleeping already. Would you prefer if I take him over to my place? Okay my dear, yes. I'll spend the night here and take him over to my place tomorrow. Are you going to stay there then? Okay dear, I love you."

She hung up the phone and broke up crying, stopping occasionally to take a deep breath. Then, she prayed out loud for a miracle, for God to spare her grandson's life.

Meanwhile, in the boy's room, Sebastian laid in bed with eyes wide open, trying to hear every word from his grandmother's conversation. All he could do was look up above him into the circling slow moving hurricane. The clouds were black more than he had ever seen before, potent and hot like tornado winds that destroy homes and people's lives. The clouds looked menacing, different than he had ever experienced them. Lightning flashed from the corners of the ceiling. His bed vibrated from the power of the thunder world overhead. Sebastian took a big breath and closed his eyes waiting for the winds to die down, yet they got as close to him as they had never been. His hair was pulled into many directions and his covers virtually took flight several times before he took hold of them.

He thought of his brother and prayed for his health to return. He had no clue what had happened to Santiago, but could get an idea that this was a very serious situation. He then thought about what his life would be if his brother wasn't there anymore, and he thought some more of his brother and the days before the accident, recollecting every moment. He remembered the day Santiago framed the sun collage picture as a birthday gift to him, and the day that he saved his brother from the hungry elevator.

The wind in the room slowly became calmer and the clouds still black as ash slowed to a complete stop in the ceiling of the room.

When he woke up the next morning, he opened his eyes and the first thing he did was to turn over to see if Santiago was in his bed, hoping that it had just been a silly nightmare caused by the ever-ominous clouds above, yet the bed had not been slept in at all. It appeared as untouched as it was the night before.

Later that morning, Blanche took her grandson over to her house which was on the outskirts of town. The house she lived in was a nice two-story duplex built by the Americans in earlier years. The house had a parlor in the front where the children could play and behind it a large living room for the adults. Everything was big in this house. Large furniture where children could get swallowed up, and a large kitchen that even fit a table for up to eight people at a time.

At the hospital, Michelle and Esteban sat outside the intensive care unit in a little private waiting area. They both looked as if they had not slept a wink the night before. Both looking down and quiet, not talking, just breathing, thinking, and waiting. Waiting for any news that could help them understand the condition of their beloved son.

Esteban noticed his friend Dr. Adames come by to check on them and he stood up to welcome him. They both walked away leaving Michelle by herself. Dr. Adames had not seen Santiago yet that morning but wanted to let them know he was going to go in and get an update from the ICU nurse. Esteban implored the doctor to help him see his son, almost breaking down from all the stress and endless waiting around.

Dr. Adames held his arm while Esteban just looked down, "Let me go find out how he is doing first, I think you know nurse Estevez, she might let you go in but it all depends on his status."

Esteban went back to wait with Michelle while Dr. Adames entered the ICU area. Esteban told Michelle the news that he might be able to see Santiago.

Inside the Intensive Care Unit, Dr. Adames stopped by the nurse's station and asked for Santiago's file, reviewing the notes while he spent some time chatting with her.

With Santiago's papers in hand, he walked all the way to the back of the room where Santiago had been placed. His little body rested there in the single bed, positioned completely flat, his left arm in a cast, and casts on both of his legs. His right arm had a variety of intravenous tubes connected to his veins, tape everywhere, and connections to various monitoring devices. The oxygen mask covered most of his face while the oxygen pump kept moving up and down pushing air into his lungs to keep him alive. He opened his status folder, flipping through pages to get a better picture of his situation. He then stood there for a moment looking at Santiago and deciding if Esteban would be able to stand seeing his son in this situation.

He then walked over to the nurse's station and called on nurse Estevez. After some discussion, they agreed it wasn't wise to allow Esteban to see his son yet.

He left to go speak to Michelle and Esteban, who both stood up with anxious expressions as he approached.

"Dr. Singh will be seeing him later and doesn't want any visitors. Your son is in critical condition and is being monitored 24-7. Only time will tell."

Michelle stood there looking at him with heavy bags under her eyes.

"I want to see my son. Can I go talk to nurse Estevez? Can you call her in here?"

The doctor moved both away from their seats and said quietly, "Please go home and rest, Santiago is in good hands here. Come back later today and I can find out if by then he is in a better position for you to see him. But please know that it is going to be difficult if he is still in ICU for anyone to see him."

On the way home, Michelle didn't say a word and only looked out of the side window, as far away as she could through her sunglasses. Esteban just drove, quietly lost in his own thoughts.

Once at the apartment, Michelle got in the shower and cried in the solitude that the private space provided. After her shower, she applied some makeup as quickly as she could while her husband bathed.

In their bedroom, she pulled clothes from her drawers and rushed to pack an overnight bag with anything she could think that she would need at the hospital.

When Esteban got out of the shower, he seemed to be taking his time which Michelle added to the list of resentments she harbored against him. She didn't say a word. She just sat there by the side of the bed, making it look like she was occupied finishing up the packing. Esteban was also quiet. Not a word came out of him until he sat down next to her on the bed.

"I don't want my son to die. This was all my fault."

He whimpered like a lost child. Michelle felt sorry for him and embraced him as he sat there anguished. After he composed himself, he called the hospital to find out any news but there was none to give.

It was not long until they were back on the road again, making a brief stop at Blanche's house to check on Sebastian. That Sunday seemed to fly by for them.

By the time they returned to the hospital, it was already five in the afternoon. Neither one noticed the day had turned gray. The behavior of the clouds mimicked those from Sebastian's room the previous night.

At the hospital waiting area they stood, sat, and paced through an additional night without news.

The next morning, Dr. Singh finally met with Santiago's parents to provide them with an update on his condition. They both sat on two chairs across from Dr. Singh in his private office.

"We have been running some tests and it appears that Santiago is not responding as we would have hoped. I will consider him not to be in a critical state at the moment, but needs constant observation."

"Can I see my son?" Asked Santiago's father.

"I wouldn't want anyone seeing him at the moment." He then gave it some thought and answered, "I know you've seen some cases working here, but this is different; he's your son."

"I want to see my son!" Esteban insisted defiantly.

"Okay, let me tell you this, I will let you go see him for just one minute, okay?"

"Yes, yes, let's go." He responded even before Dr. Singh was finished. The doctor smiled and made his eyes squint with a soulful impression. Dr. Singh then asked Esteban to go wash his face and hands clean, then was provided with a doctor's coat and a mask to cover his mouth and nose. They went into the ICU and walked to the back of the room. Dr.

Singh opened the privacy curtain and there lay Santiago's almost dead body on the bed in front of his father.

Esteban watched him the whole minute, not saying a word, or even blinking, while tears rolled down his cheeks. He was completely devastated. He couldn't believe how a small child could have been broken in so many different ways. Dr. Singh stood next to him holding Esteban with a warm embrace, then proceeded to quietly close down the curtain. As they walked away, no words were said, but the pain and suffering Esteban felt was profound. He cleared his face before walking out of the intensive care unit. Once outside, Dr. Singh went back in while Esteban removed the coat and face mask.

"Did you see him, Esteban?" Michelle asked.

"Let's take a walk, I need to get a cup of coffee." He held his wife perhaps as he never had before and walked close to her all the way outside toward an open patio with tables and chairs for employees to take their breaks.

The place was almost idyllic, with trees surrounding the circular patio and a small pond in the middle. Sun rays entered the space from the side causing stunning reflections and shadows from sculptures of colored glass that sat high above the opening of the patio. They sat at a table in a quiet area of the cafeteria and looking at her in the eyes, he proceeded to tell her what he had seen in the ICU. He kept a lot from her in order to save her the agony. He couldn't believe how the accident had left their son. She didn't say much, just shaking and holding his hands as hard as she could.

"They'll move him to a room tomorrow if the swelling in his head goes down." He didn't know what else to say.

On the way back to their apartment, Michelle told her husband that she couldn't stay there and suggested they stayed at Blanche's house instead so that they could be with Sebastian. He agreed.

At the apartment, she went in the bathroom and with an old tooth brush she had in the cabinet under the sink, she washed Santiago's shoes clean from the blood and stains caused by the accident. More tears were lost as the harder she cleaned, the worst it felt. She then took a towel from the towel hanger next to her and dried the shoes inside and out. She walked into the boys' room and conscientiously placed the shoes on the side of Santiago's bed facing the door. She stood there looking at the shoes for some time, then her eyes moved around the room, ending on the other side of the room where Santiago's new guitar rested sitting upright against the wall.

They packed a bag with clothes for several days and

drove to Blanche's house. It was two or three in the afternoon by then when Blanche opened the door and let her daughter and son-in-law in her home. Sebastian went running to the door as he had not heard from his parents except for what Blanche shared with him.

They sat in the dining room where Michelle provided edited news about Santiago with her mother. Blanche held a hand-stitched cloth napkin in one of her hands and as she heard the updates, she would bring it up to her nose holding back tears to avoid alarming Sebastian.

"Where is Santiago, Mom?" Asked Sebastian.

"Well, he is still in the hospital but they are taking great care of him, since your daddy works there and everyone knows him."

Her son then asked, "Is he going to be all right?"

"We hope so Sebastian. We certainly hope so, son." Esteban gently replied.

"Let's go to church at the six o'clock service and pray for your brother, why don't we?" Everyone agreed.

"Go back to watch TV, son."

That afternoon, Michelle seemed to be on the phone for several hours giving updates to friends and family about her son's condition.

Later on, several of Michelle and Esteban's friends

stopped by to give them emotional support. The Hendricks, who never missed a party, arrived first. Hank, Esteban's best friend was there as well. Justine and Camilla came by and a few others too. Blanche ordered take out for the visitors and offered them orange soda which she always had chilling in her refrigerator for when her grandkids visited. Sebastian and Camilla watched the television set in the guest bedroom while the adults chatted. They could sometimes hear Michelle crying out loud, especially when someone arrived at the house.

Camilla asked her cousin if Santiago was going to get well, to which he answered that he wasn't sure. No one had really said anything to him about the accident other than the little he heard from the boy that came to the house to give them the news and what he overheard at the hospital. He shared what he knew with Camilla and all she could do was cover her mouth in shock.

"Poor little Santiago." That's all she said.

That evening, everyone accompanied the family to the church where the priest prayed for Santiago's health.

Early Wednesday morning, Santiago was moved to the seventh floor to a private and quiet room close to a nurse station. Michelle and Esteban arrived at the hospital an hour later when visiting hours were allowed. This time, they brought Sebastian with them hoping that he could see his brother. They got out of the elevator and stopped at the check-in desk where they signed in. An older nurse sitting behind the desk, while looking at Sebastian, disclosed out loud that the child could not go in the room to visit with the patient. He looked up at his parents with a worried expression on his face.

"Why can't I see my brother?"

On their way to Santiago's room, Esteban and Michelle explained to Sebastian that his brother was still asleep and the nurse didn't want him to be awakened. So they walked down the hall with light yellow painted walls toward a room across from a long tall desk that Sebastian couldn't reach. Outside of the room there were three chairs. Michelle asked her son to sit on one of the chairs and wait there while they went in the room.

She opened the door softly as she usually did in the mornings when she went into her children's room to check on them. The room was dark. The curtains had been drawn, with only a sliver of sun light coming through. Her husband sat on the first chair inside of the room next to the door, directing his eyes toward his son. Michelle walked over to Santiago as if he was just sleeping on his own bed, quietly feeling the space of the bed with her hand. She didn't know how to react. She could hear the noise from the oxygen machine and beeping sounds that took over the otherwise quiet room. By now, Santiago's head inflammation had receded but he still had bruises all around his head and parts of his face. He was lying on his back in the same position as he was when Esteban saw him in the ICU two days before. She clutched Santiago's right hand softly and held it for as long as she could. His hand was cold and flaccid. She looked at her son and tried to process how someone could do this to a child.

A nurse walked in and changed an almost empty IV bag while Michelle asked the nurse about his state, to which she replied with a kind smile that he was stable, not offering further information. She then reminded them about the visiting hours ending at 11:30 am.

Esteban stood up and walked outside to check on Sebastian, who was sitting there just looking around while his legs swung back and forth. His father walked over to the tall desk in front of the room and said something to one of the people behind the counter. He was given a packet which he brought over to Sebastian.

"Here is a coloring kit to entertain yourself for now."

"Can I see Santiago. Can I go in?"

His father knelt next to him and responded in a sad

tone, "Sebastian, he is not doing well. He is not responding and I'd hate for you to see him like that. The accident left him very bruised. Would you like to see him like that?"

"I just want to see how he's doing."

"He's going to be okay." His father got up from the eye level position to his son and stumbled as he stood up. Sebastian offered his hand for his dad to grab on but he refused to hold it and almost fell backwards. He appeared to be upset and walked away toward another hallway.

After about fifteen minutes of Sebastian sitting around, he set aside the page he was coloring and looked up toward the door of his brother's room. He noticed there was a window on the door itself that he could look into. He watched to see if anyone was around and got up slowly. As he was getting out of the chair, he saw a nurse walk by and go into the nurse's station. He got back into his seat almost knocking out the coloring pencils on the chair next to him. He stayed there on his chair which was a good thing because minutes later, his aunt arrived holding hands with Camilla. When they saw Sebastian sitting in the waiting chairs, they rushed over to greet him. Camilla asked how Santiago was doing. He responded that he wasn't allowed to go in the room. Aunt Justine looked at him from where she was standing and asked, "Where's your mom?"

"She's inside in the room." As Justine walked in the room, both children got up and stood behind her to see if they could get a glimpse of Santiago but were surprised to see that a screen had been placed in front of the door and only darkness could be seen inside. The little bit of light that Sebastian was able to capture came from the light above Santiago's bed, but nothing more. As the door closed behind Justine, the children walked back to their seats and waited around.

"They haven't said anything to you about Santiago?" Asked Camilla.

"No." Answered Sebastian.

"Mommy was telling someone on the phone that Santiago was just playing in the sidewalk and was hanging on a branch acting like a monkey when the lady drove on the sidewalk by where he was. He fell on the windshield of the car breaking it and the woman took off with him on top. I don't know how he ended up on the street but he was stuck under the car and dragged under it." They both sat there quiet after that looking down not understanding the meaning of the situation.

That Wednesday night, Sebastian and his parents went back to Blanche's house. Sebastian's father took off without explanation. Michelle had a good cry with her mother while Sebastian stayed in his room doing homework that had been left for him by his teachers since he was absent from class since Monday.

That night, after homework, Blanche prepared turkey sandwiches for the three of them. Sebastian asked his mother when he was going to be able to see his brother, but she gave him yet another excuse for not being able to see him.

That evening, he went to bed confused and lonely as he had ever felt. The room he was staying in at his grand-mother's house was quite cold, bare, and very different to the bedroom he shared with his brother at home. There was a single bed pushed to one corner of the room and an old desk full of dust and office things that had been around since he could remember. His little luggage laid there next to the bed.

That night he went to bed thinking about something else Camilla said to him that made him feel incredibly unsettled. She said that perhaps Santiago would not live and if he did, he would be a vegetable. So there that night, he looked up at the ceiling of this undecorated room, at the never-ending whirlpool of light and clouds rushing around the room from corner to corner, and from one side to the other. While he looked at all of it, he asked himself what would life be without his brother. Since he could remember, he had a brother and since he could remember, he had a companion he could talk to at night that would protect him from whatever daunting thing waited outside their room. He then started to recollect memories from the past of all the fights, and games, and conversations he ever had with his brother. And as he reminisced and wondered about the unknowns of his future, he fell asleep and so did the clouds above him.

On Thursday, Sebastian and his parents went back to the hospital together and waited there without any news of Santiago. Michelle mentioned that a nice nurse had brought a wooden cross and placed it on the wall above Santiago's bed in the hospital room and that this spiritual blessing brought her much comfort.

Sebastian stayed at his grandmother's house all day Friday and didn't see his parents that night. He received a telephone call from his mother that evening saying that they were going to be late and to follow his grandmother's directions for going to bed early. She appeared to be particularly melancholic in the way she spoke to her son that Friday. He asked her to give Santiago a hug for him.

After dinner, he changed into his favorite pajamas and watched some cartoons that evening before getting into bed. Not seeing his brother for six days, or his parents for a full day, was starting to take a toll on him. He still didn't understand what was happening to his brother and wondered once again what it would feel like to not have him in his life. There he laid at around one in the morning when Blanche woke him up shaking him softly.

"Is everything okay?" She asked him.

Sebastian not grasping what she was talking about asked, "Yes, I am okay, what happened?"

"I don't know, I heard thunder. Almost like the sound of earthquake coming from the room. I thought something had fallen." She replied.

He yawned and said, "No grandma, everything's fine."

She got up from the bed, looked around still baffled and walked out of the room, closing the door behind her. As soon as his grandmother left the room, Sebastian felt the rush of an overwhelming gust from a huge hurricane swirl above him. He had never seen anything like this before. He could see through the storm clouds as if they were made out of clear glass and there were search lights everywhere. Past the spinning clouds, in a different layer, were the stars and galaxies in front of an infinite black background of stars and a huge sun-like shape in the center of the ceiling high above him. It was like the ceiling had come off the room. The sheet covering his body flew off swiftly and onto the opening above him. He sat on his bed looking up wondering what was so different this time. The more he focused toward the center of the storm, he could feel the warm humid air rush through the room and around him as if wanting to envelope him and take him away like in the tornado scene from *The Wizard of Oz*. Scared from what was occurring in the room and alone without his brother there to protect him, he wrapped himself in a fetal position while covering his face and his head in case anything would fall on him. The harsh wind blew past him and got even closer than it had ever. The noise was overwhelming. It was indeed as if a smokeless tornado was pulling him off the bed. He could hear the rush of wind gusts moving around him and picking up his shoes, socks, and knick-knacks sitting on the old desk in the other corner of the bedroom. He then felt this incredibly deep thrust of energy come to him from deep within and opened his eyes as a valiant soldier, gazing wide to realize his body was completely off the bed and suspended in mid-air between the mattress and the ceiling. He didn't feel scared anymore. He was levitating and he could feel this rush of wind blowing from below that kept him stable without falling or flying up into the span of space above him. His body kept moving upward above the ceiling slowly and as he passed the clear clouds of the rushing hurricane structure, he felt complete stillness in the air as if he had entered a different stratum. In this new layer, he saw the stars and the space more clearly above him with planets far away surrounding the sun all the way on the very center. He could also view the milky way and other galaxies further away. The light of the sun appeared bright and clear to the point that Sebastian could even see the sun spots and sunbursts as he had never seen them before. Looking at the sun wouldn't burn his eyes either. From the inside of the sun he began seeing a series of shapes that became clearer the longer he stared at them. Santiago's face became sharper and fully into view. His face had a pleasant smile and his green eyes looked greener and brighter than they had ever been before. As Sebastian suspended there in mid-air, he unexpectedly felt a rush of peace and from the corner of his left eye, coming from the west toward the east, he encountered a shooting star that moved slowly and bright across space.

"Sebastian, wake up."

Sebastian opened his eyes and saw his father there sitting on the side of his bed.

"Sebastian, I have some news, you need to get up."

Sebastian removed the bed sheet covering him and sat down next to his dad. Confused and wondering what was going on he asked, "What happened, Dad?"

"It's ten o'clock, you've slept a long time. I have to tell you something. Santiago … died last night in his sleep."

Sebastian just sat there not understanding. The words didn't make sense and certainly didn't belong together in the same sentence. It was not something that he had ever thought of or expected to ever happen.

"What's the matter with you? You're not going to cry for your brother? Your brother just died."

Sebastian didn't know what to do. He was in shock and didn't know how to react. Scared of his father, not knowing what to do, he forced himself to cry or at least act as if he was crying. His father didn't have a clue that children didn't understand these things. Sebastian had never dealt with death before and the news were extremely unsettling.

After a few minutes his father said calmly, "He now rests in peace and he didn't suffer."

His father hugged him with one of his large arms while looking away. Sebastian was pushed toward his dad being forced to hug him back. They stayed there for some time, together, alone in the room, considering the news and how difficult it must have been for his father to share them with his now only living son.

"Go get in the shower and get ready because a lot of people will come over today." His dad got up and walked out together with Sebastian so that he could go into the bathroom that was just across from the bedroom.

In the bathroom, while he took a shower, he reflected on the news that his father had given him. He couldn't really process the fact that his brother had died. He could only understand it in a physical manner. His brother was no longer there which meant that he would be alone in his bedroom moving forward. He thought that he would not have anyone to fight with anymore, and he thought about how much space there would be in the car now that Santiago wasn't there. He then realized that he would not have anyone to talk to at nights when the lights went out in their room or someone to protect him when he needed to go to the bathroom in the middle of the night. He never considered what it meant to die, to not live anymore and what that really meant.

Sebastian got dressed and scared of what to expect, walked out slowly toward Blanche's living room trying not to make any noise. His aunt Justine who was sitting closer to him got up from the sofa and gave him a warm hug that seemed to last forever. His mom was sitting next to

Justine. She called him by extending her arm to him. She grabbed him and hugged him profoundly as he fell on the sofa between her and Justine.

There were other people there, all dressed in black, half of them he didn't know. Camilla, who was in the kitchen with Blanche, walked back into the living room noticing that Sebastian was awake. She ran over to hug him. Esteban stayed in the kitchen with Hank and some of the other men while the women and kids stayed around the front of the house. Michelle cried quietly sitting there, not knowing what to do, sometimes saying incoherent things.

"The day before the accident he came out of nowhere and gave me this huge squeeze and said that he loved me, as if he knew he was going to be taken away from us."

Then she would say things like, "Why would a woman drive up on the curb and hit a child, then try to escape the scene? He would have survived if she didn't try to run away from the accident."

Justine, in order to avoid having the children hear any more of this responded, "Michelle, we can't change what has happened."

Michelle gave Justine a dirty look and looked away. Justine felt upset and got up to the kitchen. Michelle sat there with her son who still didn't understand the severity of the situation. He expected that his brother would come home any moment and prove everyone wrong.

More people visited Blanche's house that day including some of Santiago's friends, neighbors, Michelle's school colleagues, and others. Some people brought covered dishes with food for the family and some brought envelopes that were handed to his parents. They spent hours on end in the living room chatting, sometimes remarking about how Santiago was this, or Santiago was that. Sebastian sat there listening and sometimes smiling about the artificial jokes that some of the adults would tell to lighten the mood. But it was horribly apparent that it was not a cheerful moment. Sebastian's head ached as if it had been thrown in a blender, confused and lost.

The family stayed at Blanche's that night after having their last visitors leave that Saturday evening. Sebastian went back into the empty bedroom and changed into his pajamas. His parents slept in one of the spare bedrooms next to Sebastian's and that night it was him who tucked his parents to bed. He walked in their bedroom and wished them a good night. Michelle, whose face was red and swollen from so much crying, hugged her child as tight as she could and wished him a good night. His father did the same and asked, "Are you going to be okay by yourself?"

"Yes, Dad." He responded while walking out.

In his bedroom, everything was inexplicably in order as if nothing had ever happened the night before. He didn't question any of it however, since he had already taken way too much for one day. He closed the door of the room and looked at how far it was to the bed, then quickly turned the light switch off and in a couple of skips he landed in the bed. There, in the complete darkness of night he turned toward the wall and shed tears for everything that had happened that day and that whole week. His body and mind couldn't take the stress any longer. He then looked up expecting his confident swirl of clouds companion but found an empty white ceiling with an unassuming light fixture in the center, nothing more. There were no clouds rumbling about above him, no whirlpools, no hurricanes. He didn't quite try to understand the meaning of this. The only thing he could do was close his eyes. And as he rested there, falling slowly asleep, he peeked at the ceiling once more but it was still the same; black as the dark side of the sun.

Santiago was laid to rest on Tuesday, November twenty-third. The morning service was to take place at ten, followed by the funeral procession to the cemetery. Sebastian was dressed in a white long sleeve shirt with a black tie, black pants, and his black school shoes. When they parked at the church, they saw that many guests had arrived, including Camilla and Justine. They got out of the car and all walked into the church together. Sebastian looked around to see if he could see where his brother was. When he looked down toward the altar, he saw a little white box by the side and wondered if he was there. They all walked toward the front and pointed at the area where they would all sit. There were so many people at the church by the time the service started that many had to stand in the halls. Sebastian and his parents sat on the first row of benches and waited for guests to stop by offering their condolences. Some of the visitors would go over to the white box and would touch it and make the sign of the cross. Sebastian sat there wondering about the whole activity while people stopped, chatted with his parents for a moment, then looked down at him with sorrow. Sebastian kept looking at the box in front of him and asked his mother if he could go see his brother.

Michelle responded, "Yes son, you should go say goodbye because from here we are going to the cemetery and you won't get another chance."

They both stood up and approached this modest box covered in a white silky fabric. Sebastian became nervous, not understanding how his brother could fit in such a small box. As he got closer in, he saw the box had a little opening covered in glass, a window to look inside. When he reached the box, he touched it and it felt harsh and cheap, but he didn't question it. He was mostly stunned that he could see this opening and as he got closer to it, he saw Santiago's face as if he was in a frozen sleep. He was wearing a white shirt with a large collar and a tie that appeared too big.

It was here when Sebastian comprehended the meaning of death, that his brother was dead. He looked at his brother and in his mind tried to take a mental picture of his face. Then he leaned as close as he could over his face, and with his eyes closed he said to him as a secret, "I love you, Santiago." He opened his eyes again to see his brother's face one last time, and by now with tears falling over the window opening, he noticed there was cotton inside of Santiago's nostrils and inside of his mouth. Part of his face was scratched and bruised on the cheek. Sebastian couldn't stop crying and through the tears that flooded his eyes, he leaned once again and gave Santiago a kiss through the glass. His mother who was completely devastated by this, held her son and tried to take him away but he had grabbed onto his brothers casket not letting go and screamed, "My brother! My brother!" He kept screaming at the top of his lungs until he was worn out, finally accepting that his brother was undeniably deceased.

Otelo and Carly, friends of Esteban, helped Michelle to move Sebastian away from the casket and toward the back of the church by the side hall. Everyone at the church could hear the painful cries of the boy as he continued screaming. "Don't take him! Don't take him!"

Everything around Sebastian moved in slow motion. Sebastian in his mind couldn't fathom that his brother was inside of that inexpensive wood box and that he would be put under the ground at a cemetery. It was not acceptable that this could happen to his brother.

He tried to get away from the adults holding him but he couldn't. Someone pulled him outside of the church as he heard his parents talking about taking him home. All he saw through the tears were faces looking at him with empathy in their eyes for they deeply felt for his loss and discomfort. Some lowered their heads and holding tissues wiped tears off their faces as he passed by.

Once in the car, Otelo, who was a pharmacist at the hospital where Esteban worked, and his wife put Sebastian on the back seat of their maroon Pontiac and drove him over to Blanche's house.

On the way there, Sebastian continued screaming and

asking Otelo to stop the car. The screaming turned into painful sobbing.

"I don't want to see my brother put away under the ground. Don't put him in the cemetery. I don't want to see that. Don't let me see him in the cemetery. Please!"

He wasn't sure where he was going after all. Through his anxiety attack he couldn't comprehend his brother being dropped in a hole and left there. He continued sobbing as he jumped up and down in the back seat of the car all the way to his grandmother's house, possessed by the deeply painful realization about his brother. Otelo and Carly felt the poor boy's agony and didn't utter a word through the whole trip as they dealt with the loss in their own way.

Once they arrived at Blanche's, a lady who had been hired to help opened the door and let Sebastian and the adults in the house. Sebastian took off running into his temporary bedroom and locked himself in. He took off the tie that was preventing him from breathing and fell on the bed on his stomach and continued to grieve hysterically. The pain intensified even more every time he had the vision of his brother's face behind the layer of glass in the casket. The more he remembered his face, the more frenetic his anguish became. He heard knocking on the door but didn't care who it was on the other side. He just laid there sobbing some more and feeling like the earth was going to swallow him. Santiago's face kept appearing in his mind and his desperation for accepting the truth of his life became too hard to manage.

The door opened and the woman at the house came in followed by Otelo who had a pill and a glass of water for Sebastian. He called to Sebastian and asked him to take the medicine, reassuring him that it would help him calm down. Sebastian kept weeping which made it difficult for him to breathe at times. He swallowed the pill and drank some of the water between breaths. He laid back on the bed while Otelo sat on the side of the bed making sure that Sebastian would be alright.

After a few minutes, Sebastian was able to calm down and sleep.

It was already dark in the room. It was also dark outside the tall window behind Sebastian when he woke up later that evening. He looked out and saw that the street light was on, as well as lights from passing cars and he felt immediately disoriented as to where he was and why he was there. There seemed to be some commotion still in the house from what he could hear.

His mother walked in and noticed that Sebastian was

finally awake. Without turning the light on, she asked her son, "How are you doing, my baby? I know it was not a good day for any of us. How do you feel?"

"I'm tired, Mom." He thought for some time while his mom sat next to him and caressed his hair.

"I don't understand how Santiago could fit in that small box. I can't believe he is gone." He thought some more and asked, "Where did he go, Mom?"

He started to cry.

"His soul is with God. He took Santiago because he needed more angels in heaven. He's an angel now, Sebastian sweetheart." She was quiet and without energy from the hard day that she had endured. She had not been able to eat a bite at all in days either. Michelle then in an effort to make her flesh and blood feel better asked him if he wanted to eat something.

"Yes, Mom, I could eat."

"Okay, let's go get a bite, there are a lot of leftovers."

She held his hand and both walked out to the living room together while Blanche warmed up the food.

Sol Somnium

We wouldn't be here if it wasn't for the sun, its distance from earth and the perfect balance of elements in our planet. The sun to me represents a power that is bigger than anything anyone else may believe in. After a span of a week, when our lives changed so drastically, I began to realize that there are powers like that of the sun that I will never understand.

A week after the funeral proceedings, Esteban decided to return to the apartment with his family to try to put their lives in order again after the horrible tragedy. The next Sunday, at nine in the evening when the streets had settled from the weekend traffic, Esteban drove his family to the apartment with all the luggage and a hamper with additional clothes, boxes filled with medical and legal documents, and left-over food. On the way home, as they drove on a quiet street about a mile from home, a car ran a stop sign right in front of them almost crashing into their Volkswagen. Esteban was so furious, he got out of the car and screamed at the middle age driver in the other car.

"You ran the stop sign, you son of a bitch! Not only did a crazy bitch kill one of my sons last week, now you want to kill the rest of my family? Asshole! Get off the roads, you shouldn't be allowed to drive!"

The man held his arms up apologetically and responded, "I am so sorry sir, I didn't see the stop sign."

The man quickly got back in his car and took off on his way. Meanwhile in the car, Michelle and their son watched what happened in front of their eyes in shock, both almost lacking any more feeling inside.

When Esteban got back in the car, he was shaking like a leaf from the trauma of what he had just experienced.

He questioned if it was meant to be that God wanted to take his family away and wondered if he was just being punished for not being there for them. His wife extended her arm over his back caressing it and reassuring him. "Nothing happened. Let's go home."

When Esteban opened the door of the apartment, it smelled musty like the beach house of vacations past. The home felt empty and desolate, as though it had also suffered Santiago's loss. Sebastian sat in the living room for some time looking around while his parents brought things into the kitchen. His dad looked at him sitting there and asked him to help, which he did right away.

After everything had been brought into the house, Sebastian walked to the bedroom he shared with his brother for so many years and studied it to see if perhaps everything that just happened was only part of his imagination. Santiago could be hiding in the room all this time and he would show up and surprise him as he usually did when they played hide and seek. The room was dark and quiet. Only a little bit of light came into the room as clouds had been forming outside for an expected rainstorm. The shoes that Santiago wore the day of the accident were there sitting by his bed where his mother had placed them. The guitar that Santiago had been learning to play sat in a corner of the room, where he placed it last.

Sebastian opened the closet doors and when he saw some of Santiago's clothes, he couldn't handle it anymore and began to scream and cry again. His mom was there behind him, following him like a shadow, and before he could fall on the floor, she was there to catch him. She brought him onto his bed and sat there holding him for as long as she could.

His father stood outside of the room looking in at the bed that belonged to Santiago and all the memories of his past. He just stood there, with a blank empty expression, then walked out into his own room.

Late that night, as Sebastian rested on his bed, he looked over at his brother's bed, wishing for him to come in from playing and get back into bed. He tried not to blink to see if Santiago would appear from under the bed and scream "Surprise!"

After an hour or more of waiting, tossing, and turning, Sebastian began to cry quietly some more, and as he did, he turned his head to look up at the ceiling, bed sheets covering him to his nose just as he used to do. He looked around for the gray clouds that had called the ceiling their home for so long, yet the clouds were not there. He looked from one corner to the other, but the clouds had disappeared. He closed and rubbed his eyes to see if this would help them return but the clouds didn't come back at all.

When he opened them again, he felt cold as if he was inside of a gray fluffy cloud. The fog filled his room and he couldn't see past his hands. The air was so humid, he could feel the water stick to his arms and face. He looked over to see if he could see Santiago's bed but it wasn't there. He looked behind him and realized that he wasn't in his bed either, he was now standing up. Upon looking around he found a light source coming to him directly at the front. As the fog dissipated, he slowly began to see, hear, and smell things that felt familiar to him. First came the sounds of the ocean waves splashing in front of him. Then, he smelled the ocean and the flowers he was so enamored of when his family went on vacation at the beach. Slowly, things began to appear sharper, and the walls, windows, and closets of his room became more visible around him. He looked behind him and saw the framed sun collage on the wall behind his bed. Then something distracted him from further examining the space he was in. He began to hear a rumble from the light source in front of him. He thought it to be the sun. He didn't quite understand this, but followed along to see what would happen next.

"Are you listening, Sebastian?" Faintly asked an agitated

Santiago who appeared to be speaking from the direction of the sunlight.

"Wha . . . ? What . . . are you doing? Where are you? I can't see you." Asked Sebastian looking around to see if he could find his brother through the dissolving mist.

"What do you mean? Can I finish now?" Santiago's face slowly appeared from within the light.

"Remember when the sun went to China through the ocean? Now it is coming back to where you are. The sun pushed its way up from the ocean causing a huge wave, and that is why we have ocean surf. The rumbling was the sun burning to come up through the Pacific Ocean and just as it popped in before, it popped up into the sky to come visit you. Lots of clouds burned off in the sky when the sun came up from China that day. Don't be scared, nothing will happen to you."

The light source in front of him grew so large, almost as if it were right there in front of Sebastian's nose but he couldn't touch it or feel its powerful energy. It was so big that it filled his bedroom. Sebastian studied Santiago's face as it became clearer and noticed no bruises. His hair was as golden and his eyes were as green as a new grass in spring.

"I never got to tell you a sun story. Can I go on?"

Sebastian nodded quickly in agreement.

"So, the sun collage you created popped up into the sky and all the birds got so stunned, they flew off and away from it. The sun and the birds all looked like the paper cutouts you made for your school sun collage. There were colorful Toucans and Macaws flying about surrounding the sun, followed by beautiful canaries and bright green parrots. The birds fluttered around in unison similar to marching bands following the pace of their music. I think you called it *The Dance of Harp and Strings* which brought you real pleasure when you heard it the first time from one of mom's records. Then just like when we hit fast forward on the tape recorder; flowers, leaves, butterflies, and ladybugs all made out of paper began to spring out from around the sun creating the most beautiful pattern that filled the heavens above."

By now, the fog had dispersed and Sebastian could see his brother's face clearly coming from the light source ahead of him. He could actually feel Santiago in the room. Sebastian tried to extend his hand to hug him but a strange force kept him from raising his arms just like the feeling he got when his arms fell asleep and weighed a million pounds. Sebastian opened his eyes and wiped tears away. He was lying in bed facing the ceiling. He quickly sat on the mattress to look ahead toward the row of windows to see if his brother was still in the room but he was not there.

Living in the apartment became more difficult every day, especially for Sebastian who had to deal with sleeping in the bedroom he had shared with his brother since he could remember. A memory-filled room. Everywhere he looked or whatever he touched felt the innocence of the loss that he was forced to assimilate in such a short period of time. His parents were also invested in those memories making it difficult to live within those walls. Everything there had Santiago's soul neatly wrapped around it.

At nights, Sebastian would cry himself to sleep quietly in his bed so that no one would hear him, and now that the cloud apparitions above him were gone, he felt the room to be stricken from all life even more. He dared not open his eyes when he faced his brother's bed anymore to avoid hurting even more. After all, his bed was still made up as if he would walk in any minute.

The apartment became such a vessel of painful memories that they decided to move to Blanche's house while they built a new home in the Altos del Chase neighborhood, a new community that was under development in 1977.

Once they were settled at Blanche's, Sebastian began to handle his brother's passing in a more manageable way.

But then, there was the wrenching return to school that both Michelle and Sebastian had to overcome.

A week after moving to Blanche's, they made the drive to school. That morning, no one said a word in the car. They were deep in their own thoughts, wondering how it would feel to return to school where Sebastian's brother also attended. He questioned how his brother's schoolmates responded to the news of Santiago's passing.

Once at school, they got out of the car and Michelle walked alongside her son into the campus. Sebastian trembled inside and out from the anxiety and felt like everyone was looking at them. All he could do was look down as he walked into the administration office following his mother in order to distract from all the attention. It felt like the longest distance for Sebastian, he just wanted to run back to the car and hide. He saw his schoolmates and others he didn't even know reach out to him and pat his back while giving him their condolences. All he could do was nod while he shed a few tears that brought back the memory of his brother's face inside of the coffin.

Once the bell rang that morning, his mother walked him into his classroom where everyone was waiting quietly for him. The teacher welcomed Sebastian back and proceeded to start her class to avoid making him more uneasy than he already was. Michelle waved at the teacher and children while she walked down the hallway to her own classroom.

Sebastian returned home exhausted from the tension felt to the further reality that now his life had changed forever even in school. He no longer had a brother that would go to the same school with him anymore. Everything was a completely new experience for him, from eating alone at times to having no one to talk to at night before falling asleep.

Months passed and the house his parents began to build started to take shape. Every time they visited the construction site, they found new walls up.

Michelle, who had started a photography hobby to keep her mind occupied, took pictures of every step of the building and kept a nicely laid out photo album.

During the visits to the building site, she noticed that Sebastian had become much more introverted and emotionally muted. To help him with the grieving process, she decided to take him to a psychologist at the hospital where Esteban worked. After a few visits, the doctor discussed his concerns with Sebastian's parents and prescribed for their son to participate in activities to help him reconnect with his family and friends.

Michelle, who had been toying with ceramics for her own distraction, offered the idea for him to make his own. She began to take him to classes on Saturday mornings once her husband disappeared to the bars. Sebastian got to enjoy playing with ceramics and created a few items that helped him occupy his mind and open up with others around him.

Slowly, Michelle began to see a positive change in herself and in her son. She celebrated his accomplishments, and she could see him enjoying himself.

As the next November approached, the memory of Santiago became evident even more for the family. For the anniversary of his passing, the family went to church to pray for his soul. There, Camilla and the rest of the family sat together in two rows. For Sebastian, the memory of the church and what had transpired a year before was still too raw in his mind and had a difficult time sitting through the service. Everyone cried that day including Camilla who became much closer with her cousin.

One day, Michelle arrived home alone crying, holding her purse covered in dirt. She sat in the living room looking toward the kitchen feeling completely hysterical, everyone in the house came running to find out what had happened. She began to cry even harder, making it hard to understand anything she said. "I was . . . robbed . . . at the cemetery."

Blanche asked her urgently, "What happened, mija?"

Michelle replied, "I went to put new flowers on Santiago's grave and suddenly I felt someone pulling my purse. The kid could have been no older than 17 at the most. He stole the money in my wallet. Thankfully, he threw the purse as he escaped."

She continued to cry like a little girl while Blanche caressed her head.

"Sebastian, can you bring her a glass of water, darling?"

He ran into the kitchen and brought her a cold glass of water and a napkin so that she could wipe off the tears and perspiration from her face.

That night, Esteban never went home until early in the morning. Everyone wondered where he was, but at this point, Michelle didn't care anymore.

Michelle, who visited her son at the cemetery once a week was robbed three times and it became such a difficult situation that she talked Esteban into moving their son's remains to a crypt at the Santuario Nacional.

The day they exhumed his remains and brought them

back to the church, the family attended church service and had the priest bring Santiago's remains to the crypt under the church with a special prayer.

Michelle continued to visit her son every week, now in the safety that the church provided and she replaced the flowers on the front of the crypt every time she went.

For Sebastian, it was difficult to visit his brother's grave and even when he was moved to the crypt. Reading his brother's name on the crypt covering made him weep from the pain of how much he missed him.

By that November they were finally able to move into their new home. The construction took ten months and everyone seemed satisfied with the results. By then, tensions between Esteban and Blanche had grown to an impossible state from his continued drinking and exposing his family to severe fights.

The day of the move, Sebastian helped bring his things into his new bedroom. He ran into his room on the second floor and carefully discovered the new carpeting, the windows looking out toward the back of the house and all the closets he now had. He dropped all his boxes and began to quickly put everything in order while the movers brought his bed frame, the mattress, and his desk into the room as well as the rest of the furniture. Sebastian made sure that Santiago's guitar sat at a prominent corner of the room to be able to see it from his bed at night.

Everything smelled like new, even the old furniture. Sebastian thought that everything looked different, much happier, in this house.

Esteban was always present for home cooked meals but once he was done, he would leave to go to his bar drinking with friends. No one could ask him where he was going or when he would be back. He was home to pay the bills but that was pretty much it. He began to drink more heavily at home and everywhere they went, especially at parties. This became such a normal practice that Sebastian began to resent his father for forcing him to attend parties with them and waiting around until he was completely wasted at the end of the night.

Esteban had distanced himself so much from Sebastian that they hardly ever said a word to each other. He lacked any care to know what his son was up to or if he was doing well in school or not. The opposite happened with Michelle who to save her only living son, became overprotective of him to the point that he felt suffocated by her insistent need to make sure he was safe. He could not go anywhere without her knowing about it. He could not meet anyone new unless it was approved by her. This put an additional layer of stress on Sebastian who by now was starting to grow out of his childhood stage, more so because of what he had gone through.

Sebastian, as a teen, began to realize some things more clearly about his father's alcoholism. Michelle attempted to talk to her husband about it many times, but this would end up in very upsetting fights that Sebastian couldn't handle anymore. Michelle even tried to have Sebastian talk to his dad about his drinking and that turned into a much bigger brawl.

His father screamed at his son, "I wish it would have been you that died instead of Santiago. Don't tell me how to live my life!"

Sebastian looked at him with angry tears in his eyes and shrieked as loud as he had ever, "I hate you," and stormed out. Esteban never apologized to his son.

A month after they had moved in the new house, across the hall in his parent's bedroom, Esteban sat on the bed, drunk and dirty from having been disloyal to his wife earlier that night. It was about one in the morning, and Michelle was already asleep having taken a pill to help the insomnia that emerged after her son's death and all the challenges she was having to deal with alone about her husband. Esteban felt emptiness in his heart, after all he wasn't very close to it. He wasn't familiar with true love and passion for life as his wife and children were. He began to cry irrepressibly but trying not to wake up his spouse.

Unexpectedly, he heard a loud boom coming from his son's bedroom. He jumped when he heard the sound and hastily walked over to investigate. Sebastian lied awake on his bed looking up disoriented and wondering what had happened. His father walked over to his bed and sat next to him, turned on the lamp on the side table and asked, "Did you hear that noise?"

"Yes, it woke me up. What happened?" Asked his boy.

Esteban looked around the room to see if something had fallen on the floor, and as his eyes focused on Santiago's guitar in the corner of the room, he noticed something rather unusual about it. He got up and walked over to the guitar, grabbed it and brought it over to the bed to inspect it under the light.

"One of the guitar strings snapped!" Said Esteban as his eyes gazed toward Santiago's picture on Sebastian's bedside table.

"Wow, really?" Sebastian responded.

"Let's worry about it tomorrow morning. Go back to

sleep, good night."

He reached over to his son and gave him a kiss on the forehead, something he wasn't accustomed to doing.

His son smelled the perspiration and the usual alcohol odor of his father's breath as he moved away from him. Esteban walked out of his son's bedroom quietly putting the guitar down in the same spot it had been. He then walked into the bathroom and washed tears off his face.

The next day, Esteban made a comment to his wife about the guitar. And then as he usually did, that Saturday, he left his wife and child to go to the bar.

At bedtime, as Michelle wished Sebastian a good night, she mentioned that his father had been crying the night before and that she thought it was the reason why Santiago popped the string on the guitar as a message to his father. Sebastian agreed that there was no other possible explanation. He then said, "It was strange because all the strings were loose on the guitar."

Reflection

Today, when I wake up every morning, the first thing I see when I open my eyes is the framed photograph of my brother sitting on the nightstand. When I brush my teeth and shave, I try to find features of my brother's face on the reflection of the bathroom mirror, but I only perceive my own. I don't see my brother on the outside, on my skin, but I know that he lives deep inside of me in an incredibly profound way.

Looking at my face, my vision blurs and I grasp images of my past where my brother and I exploded a bag full of confetti in our parent's bedroom and played carnival in Rio without really understanding the consequences. I recall the good times when Santiago and I walked up the walls in the hallway, when we played the Donny and Marie Show with cousin Camilla, or when we put on plays for our neighbors. Or the days we played in the rain as the storm poured onto the street and lightning hit everywhere around us, completely disregarding our parent's directions to stay indoors when lightning hit. But it was fun and the water felt so cool and refreshing on our bodies. Or even the day Santiago tried to defy gravity by walking on the fence out back, falling and breaking his arm. I remember the days we fought about silly things or because he called me queer or girl because I was always so sensitive and effeminate. Yet, after a while we would always make up and Santiago would tell me how much he loved me and that he never meant to hurt me. The most difficult memory of all however, like a picture frozen in time, is my brother's face behind the glass window inside the little white coffin.

The memories of my brother never seem to end and they certainly never fade. At nights, I often still peek at the ceiling of my room to see if clouds emerge from it and perhaps I'll get to see my brother once again.

Santiago was my best friend, my closest confidant, my guide, and my sanctuary. And even though he is not here with *me in a physical state, he still lives in me, his love helping me to outlive the times when I was lonely, sick, sad, afraid, or scared. Even in the happier times. Santiago never seemed to be frightened by anything. And after reflecting on this for 40 years, I have come to the conclusion that my brother was never afraid to die. I think that Santiago knew his purpose. I often think that my mother is right—even though I have a hard time believing in these things—sometimes some of the people born on this earth are taken away from us early because they are the essence of an angel.*

The morning my dad woke me up to give me the news that Santiago had died, by his subsequent actions, he confirmed what he thought of me as a boy and as the man that I would become later in life. It was at that very moment when my dad showed himself to me without the mask he wore all his life for everyone. From that moment on, he was never the same father to me. Instead of being loving, kind, and understanding that I was only a boy, he just questioned why I couldn't cry for my brother. He belittled me without any care for my innocence. I didn't know what it meant to die. While my brother was in the hospital, my parents concealed the facts of his health status making it difficult to accept that my brother was gone. I wasn't allowed to see him in the hospital or to properly say goodbye before he passed. I thought he would return home eventually. When my father dropped the bomb, I went into shock and he didn't even try to comprehend the layers of complexity that those circumstances posed on a child. It was not until I saw my brother in the little coffin at the church with my very eyes that I understood reality.

My father knew that I was different, yet he always masked that truth as if it wasn't important. This brought me unimaginable pain and an emptiness inside that still lives in me today. In an effort to win my father's affection and acceptance after my brother died, I worked harder and excelled in everything I could, yet I was never good enough for him. As I grew older and faced the reality that I was gay, something I knew very early on in my life, yet my father never accepted it, often wondering why I didn't have a girlfriend instead. Of course, this was an inconvenience for him since he felt shame for having a gay son.

What people thought of him was more important than the reality. He wanted to love me with requisites but I couldn't live someone else's lie. I couldn't wear masks like he did to fake his life away to his wife, his family, and everyone else around him. I had to accept how I was brought to this earth regardless of who loved me or not. I couldn't lie to myself to make my father happy. It is my life after all. And so, slowly through the years, the resentment for his inability to love, accept, and support me grew until we became strangers.

I felt terribly bad for him because he didn't know how to love himself. I tried to help him cope with his alcoholism and philandering but there was nothing anyone could say to him. Covering that reality with a mask didn't change the fact that the problem still existed. It not only affected him, but everyone in his life. Every time my mother threatened to leave him, he promised that he would change but that only lasted a couple of weeks. He thought he was Superman and could do whatever he pleased, regardless of his marriage vows and obligations to his family, further highlighting his egotistical inclinations.

My mother on the other hand, accepted the facts of her life head on and began the process of healing right away after my brother died. She educated herself on how to grieve in a smart and positive manner but my father didn't want any part of it.

In a way to salute my brother, she displayed photos of him everywhere around the house, including the photo I still keep today on my bedside table. This helps to keep his soul and his purpose alive every day.

But that relationship was not perfect either. She overprotected me to the point that I felt imprisoned at home. We had unpleasant fights when I tried to go out with friends. She just wanted to keep me on a tight leash so that nothing would happen to me. Later on, I understood why she did that, but the damage had already been done. After leaving home, I didn't know how to do anything for myself and for a short period of time, I even felt as if I was following on my own dad's footsteps into alcoholism, drinking to the point that I couldn't stand up anymore. I quickly realized how it affected me and the people around me and I stopped the habit completely.

I cherish that my mother was there to take on the role of both parents when my dad decided to clock out of our lives and his obligations as a husband and father. She understood, accepted, and loved me, no questions asked, no requirements, just pure love.

One day not long ago, while looking in a box of old photos, I found a picture that was taken by my father that Christmas in 1976. It was a photo of my mom and me, sitting next to the Christmas tree after we had just opened our gifts in the living room after midnight. I was wearing bright blue bell bottom pants and a plaid shirt that I had received for my birthday earlier that year. Even though the picture was in black and white, I could still vividly recall the colors of the clothes I wore, perhaps as a statement to the impact my brother's death had on me. There, my mother and I sat alone next to each other, miserable, and vacant inside as we grieved for the part of our *family that had been taken away from us. In the photo, both of us are just looking blank, questioning the why behind wrecked dreams and emotions. This photograph represents the ache and the anguish we endured when Santiago died, because even though it was my father who took the photo, my mom and I were the only ones in it and the only ones in that family after Santiago died. This is what became of our lives.*

As I studied this photo of my past, I began to take comfort in many beautiful memories. I was able to have a close relationship with my brother, closer than anyone else ever had. We shared many fun times, stories, and dreams, and did entertaining and fun things that only children can think of and get away with. The dreams he had are the hardest part for me to overcome; the potential for greatness I saw in my brother to be a good honest man with the warmest heart. I can imagine that he would have had a family with many children, and it would have been a joyful home. My brother would have either owned a business or worked in a place where he would make people happy all the time. I know my brother would have loved me unconditionally, blindly, for his heart only saw goodness and he would have wanted me to be happy.

When I feel lonely, memories of my brother make me feel alive and complete inside. When things don't go according to my plans, he is always there to remind me that it is not as bad as I think. *He even pointed at his photograph on my nightstand in one of my dreams as a reminder that he is always looking out for me. To this day, he continues to be my sun in the night.*

Finally, I take satisfaction in something that happened seven days after Santiago's fall. The nurse that placed the crucifix on the wall above Santiago's bed at the hospital had a vivid dream she later shared with my mother. She dreamed that Santiago was running through the beach side. She could see and hear him play in the sand in full vibrant color, she could hear the sound of the ocean waves and even see a beautiful long wall of bougainvillea full of flowers surrounding her. Santiago appeared to her totally pure, dressed in the same clothes he had worn the day of the accident, yet he didn't have any bruises, inflammation, or broken bones, as if nothing had happened to him. When Santiago saw her, he recognized her and ran toward her in his usual passionate manner. He got really close to her ear and whispered, "Please tell my family that I am fine and that I love them very much."

The End